PARENTING KIDS WITH ADHD

A BEGINNER'S GUIDE TO HELP YOUR CHILD SELF-REGULATE, FOCUS, AND UNDERSTAND THEIR SUPERPOWER

RENATO FLAUZINO

© Copyright _2023 - All rights reserved.

The content within this book may not be reproduced, duplicated or transmitted without direct written permission from the author or the publisher.

Under no circumstances will any blame or legal responsibility be held against the publisher, or author, for any damages, reparation, or monetary loss due to the information contained within this book. Either directly or indirectly. You are responsible for your own choices, actions, and results.

Legal Notice:

This book is copyright protected. This book is only for personal use. You can't amend, distribute, sell, use, quote or paraphrase any part, of the content within this book, without the consent of the author or publisher.

Disclaimer Notice:

Please note the information contained within this document is for educational and entertainment purposes only. All effort has been expended to present accurate, up-to-date, and reliable, complete information. No warranties of any kind are declared or implied. Readers acknowledge that the author is not engaging in the rendering of legal, financial, medical or professional advice. The content within this book has been derived from various sources. Please consult a licensed professional before attempting any techniques outlined in this book.

By reading this document, the reader agrees that under no circumstances is the author responsible for any losses, direct or indirect, which are incurred as a result of the use of the information contained within this document, including, but not limited to, — errors, omissions, or inaccuracies.

BONUS

A Special Gift for you!

As a thank you for picking out this book, here is a bonus for you!

A "5 Nutrition Key Facts To Battle ADHD"

CONTENTS

Introduction	7
1. BREAKING DOWN YOUR CHILD'S ADHD:	13
What Does ADHD Mean?	14
What is the *DSM*?	18
What are the Different Types of ADHD?	21
Are ADD and ADHD Different?	25
What Causes ADHD?	26
2. UNDERSTANDING THE SUPERPOWER	28
The Importance of Acceptance	30
Trust the Power of the Mind	36
Do not Make Assumptions	40
Let Go of Perfectionism	42
3. IT ALL STARTS WITH THE PARENTS	44
Parenting an ADHD Child vs. Parenting a Neurotypical Child	44
Become a SUPER-PARENT	45
Make a Good Life for Yourself	46
Disciplining your ADHD Child	53
Mind your Own Bad Habits	68
4. ADHD ISN'T A LIMITATION	71
Learn How Motivation Works For Your Child	72
Know how the ADHD Brain Works Scientifically	76
5. TRAINING AND THERAPY	81
Types of Therapy	82
6. LET'S TALK ABOUT MEDICATION	89
How Medication Can Help in Treatment	91
Common Side Effects of Medications	92
Common Questions Regarding ADHD Medications	94
What happens to your brain on Adderall?	95
7. IT MIGHT NOT EVEN BE ADHD	101
Why is ADHD Often Misdiagnosed?	101
What Conditions Can ADHD be Misdiagnosed as?	103

8. CREATE THE PERFECT ENVIRONMENT AT HOME	108
Be Consistent: Why is Consistency at Home so Important?	108
How Aromatherapy Can Help Your Child Relax at Home	114
Nutrition: *You Are What You Eat!*	116
Teach Your Child to Be Grateful	125
9. THE IMPORTANCE OF EXERCISE	130
Balancing Exercises	133
10. MANAGING BIG FEELINGS	136
Why does ADHD make it Harder for Children to Control Their Emotions?	136
The Wall of Awful	144
11. YOUR ADHD CHILD AND DISCIPLINE... AGAIN	149
Screen Time	150
Empower What Your Kid Controls	154
Punishing your Child	164
12. DEALING THE REST OF THE WORLD	167
Making Friends	168
Dealing with Bullies	171
13. BONUS CHAPTER	178
The Illusion of Choice	178
Additional Advice for Dealing with ADHD Kids	179
14. CONCLUSION	183
My ADHD and I	185
Take Away from the Book	186
Please Review My Book	189
Acknowledgments	191
References	193

INTRODUCTION

At the best of times, being a parent is stressful. From the moment they exist, this tiny little human being depends on you for everything. EVERYTHING!

You might think you know what it feels like to be a parent, but the truth is, it's not always going to be idyllic. Try as you might, you'll not always be able to anticipate your child's every mood and whim or give them exactly what they need all the time. Being a parent is about "learning on the job"; nothing will prepare you for parenthood before you are one. Mistakes will be made no matter how much you prepare yourself or think you are ready.

It might as well be the most demanding job in the world. Now, throw into the mix a child who has ADHD, and the job suddenly becomes a thousand times more complicated!! Since you are already reading this book, let me make an educated guess. Chances are, you think they might have or do have this disorder.

You might also be a sibling, a relative, a teacher, or an educator who has come in close contact with an ADHD kid, and you want to know more about them. This is genuinely excellent news because I can tell this child means a lot to you! And let me tell you this: this child is lucky to have you!

Allow me to introduce myself at this point. Then, you can also

Introduction

understand why my book is what you are looking for! My name is Renato Flauzino, born in Curitiba, Brazil. My parents are both teachers - my mom being a pedagog and my dad an aesthetics teacher. Due to their career choices, education, schooling, and reading have always been a part of my childhood. Throughout my life, I was fortunate to have had two wonderful parents to guide me through everything.

I was a teenager when we moved to the USA to be enrolled in a high school. Let me assure you; this was very different from my life growing up. During this significant transitional period, I was also diagnosed with ADHD. To be precise, I was 14 years old at that time - a turbulent period in every boy's life. It was completely unexpected. My teachers told me I was "too much" to handle.

As you can guess, it was heartbreaking for them and me. I have very vivid memories of that time. I remember one incident when my teachers summoned my parents, who refused to acknowledge my ADHD. Instead, they said I was being "wild" out of sheer malice. As I sat there shamefaced and downcast, my unyielding teachers described how I had disobeyed them in class.

I don't think I have to tell you how low I felt the whole time, do I? But, if your child has faced bullying and misunderstanding in school, or if you have had trouble making people understand what they are going through, you'll know exactly what I am talking about.

I had always been a happy child. Compared to many people around us, we had an idyllic life. I was going through a million and a half emotions at that time of my life - the fear of failing despite trying my best, the guilt of letting down everyone around me, and the frustration at my limitations. So everything that you think that your child suffers from, I have lived through. Bitterly.

I remember thinking: why couldn't I control my anger when something I disliked happened? Why did I have to involuntarily subject myself to all the thoughts and ideas that entered my mind? Why am I always miles away when I try so desperately to stay in the moment and focus in class or follow my parent's directions?

There's one more thing I would like to add here. Despite all the hardships I was going through then, I had a constant companion with me. You see, it was not just me who had this condition, but my younger brother, Emanoel, one year younger than me and a student at that time, who was also diagnosed with dyslexia. So we were both diagnosed almost simultaneously with different severity of symptoms, making it difficult for my parents to deal with the situation.

My brother struggled to control his feelings against his best efforts; it was like he was a volcano ready to explode his emotions at any time. Like me, he also had a lot of trouble convincing other people of his ADHD. I witnessed his sadness when his friends thought he was lying about his difficulties or acknowledging his limitations. As much as I struggled, I was also scared for my brother and hurt by his pain.

Thankfully, we had our parents to get us through the dark days. Being teachers, they were aware of ADHD and after some research on how, if left untreated, it can eventually lead to more significant problems in the future. They are the inspiration behind this book. Their immeasurable patience - significantly my dad's - helped us, especially me, to accept our ADHD brains and learn to live with it. Everything we have achieved today, both my brother and I, we owe all to them. I love you, guys! You were, and always will be, the best!

My mother! Wow, she was just relentless in her journey to help me. She brought sheer energy and determination into our lives, and our education still amazes me after so many years! My parents have always said I was a gifted child. I later realized that my ADHD could have been a massive part of my gift. I am always happy to help those in need and grateful for my experiences.

I had terrific parents who understood me and tried their best to help me. With all I had to struggle with at school, I also have millions of happy memories with my family, friends, and those who loved me. Most importantly, I had my brother - my best friend and biggest companion. Even though we fought many times growing up, we helped each other because we knew what the other was going through. We made each other stronger. Even

Introduction

today, I can't imagine what I would have done to overcome that difficult time without my brother's help and support.

What prompted me to start this book is to help your child deal with ADHD and accept it so they don't grow up thinking they are defective or problematic. Or that you don't feel like you've failed as a parent just because your child fails to stay organized, or turn in their homework, when they seem to be lagging behind others, unable to control their emotions, and being disrespectful. You feel like you have tried everything to improve this, and nothing seems to work.

Because you see, having this condition doesn't mean you have a disease, neither it indicates any attention deficit. On the contrary, what these children have can only be considered an "abundance of attention." Yes, you've read it right! Their only problem is that they can't always control their attention, and that's an entirely different matter.

This can end up being your child's greatest asset, which makes them stand out from the rest of the world. Take it from me, someone who has lived with it all his life. I like to see it as your child's SUPERPOWER (Read more in chapter 5). Every child is different, and the way to deal with them must also be unique. You'll be the best to know how to manage their BIG EMOTIONS (Read more about this in Chapter 9) at all times, and I believe I can help you with that in this book.

Listen, I am not here to sugarcoat anything. Parenting a neurodivergent kid will be challenging because there will be a lot you won't be able to control. These children just happen to be different from other neurotypical ones. There's no denying that. Here are some things I went through that may sound familiar to you.

- Is your child often restless, unaware of exactly what they want?

- Do they struggle with following the rules? Do they do the opposite of what you expect them to do?

- Do they struggle to focus on anything in particular for more than a few minutes, even if they express interest in it?

Introduction

- Are they in the habit of leaving most of their chores, homework, and activities half-completed, despite your reminders?
- Do they struggle with staying organized or even functioning correctly at certain times?
- No sense of time? Frequently late and do things at the last minute?
- Well, this might all be because of their condition! But you might know that already.

As a parent, it is going to be torture sometimes. It might or might not get better with time, depending on the actions taken. Your pre-teen, teenager, or older child might be even harder to help. But remember this: if they are diagnosed early and the right treatments are used, these symptoms can eventually ease off. Unfortunately, it's hard to say if they will go away completely. There is no cure for ADHD. However, when you properly learn all the tips and tricks to manage your child's symptoms, it will be much more manageable. (Read more about how to control the symptoms in Chapter 10).

You're not alone in this! Millions of parents all over the world struggle with children who are considered "a handful," "unmanageable," or "uncontrollable" by society. With my book, I can show you some of the best ways to help your kid - methods that have proved foolproof and practical for years. I've combined techniques my parents have used, and methods my brother and I found helpful throughout our lives. It's a sum-total of my experience and knowledge about ADHD.

Here is a hint of how this guide can help you and your little one. In the following very well-researched and carefully-constructed chapters, you'll learn plenty to understand it, know if and when you should consult an expert to diagnose your kid, and many different methods to improve their symptoms, such as:

- Behavioral Therapy exercises.
- Amazing tricks and tips to improve their relationships and progress at school and home.
- Ability to control their big emotions.

Introduction

- Understand their brains and how to discipline them with the right approach.
- Working together on accepting their SUPERPOWER.
- And much, much more!

Most importantly, based on my own experiences and having the best parents in the world. You'll know precisely the kind of parent you need to be for them. What my parents were for my brother and me, you too can be the safety net for your children. To make it clear, they were not the best because they did everything perfectly. In fact, many times were the opposite, but their support, patience, and love made them the best!

You can turn your child's ADHD into their SUPERPOWER instead of their limitations. Most importantly, as a true well-wisher of your kiddos, you'll learn exactly how to act and react so they have the best possible help available. So if you often feel helpless and unsure how to help your child's fantastic brain, read ahead. You'll find the answers to all your questions here in this book.

P.S. Keep a notebook around so you can jot down anything important or anything you think might be helpful!

1
BREAKING DOWN YOUR CHILD'S ADHD:
WHAT IS IT, AND WHAT TO EXPECT

Perhaps you already have an idea of what it means to have ADHD. Still, the first step is educating yourself about this condition, so you can understand and help your child. If you have not consulted an expert but suspect your child might have ADHD, this chapter will help you the most.

For the sake of using this book as a resource, I will provide in-text citations for every technical statement I make. I don't have a degree in psychology. But I live with this disorder, and I am passionate about finding ways to cope with these symptoms that come in all different shapes and sizes. So I checked current scientific journals, studies, and experts' statements to give correct and valuable information.

First, you can't just see an extremely active child and assume they have ADHD. However, it's entirely normal for any parent to be concerned and distressed. ADHD stands for *Attention Deficit Hyperactivity Disorder. The* name became its current form in 1987 when the American Psychiatric Association (APA) released the DSM-III (Morin, 2017). It's actually a misleading name because you don't have to be hyperactive to have it.

Also, it's not that people with this condition have an attention deficit; instead, regulating their attention is difficult. In fact, they have an abundance of attention. Frank Coppola *says, "I prefer to distinguish ADD as attention abundance disorder. Everything is just so interesting... remarkably at the same time."*

Dr. Russel Barkley, an ADHD expert, gives another excellent perspective on understanding what it feels like to have this disorder. *"It's not an attention disorder, it's an executive disorder"* (2012). Executive function is a set of mental skills that enable a person to self-control, plan ahead, focus despite distractions, and remember and follow instructions. No one is born with such skills, but most of us, some more than others, can develop these skills depending on our experience throughout childhood into adolescence (Center on the Developing Child at Harvard University, 2020).

It can be first diagnosed in children around 3 years old, depending **on the severity and how often the symptoms affect everyday life,** according to Brown (2021). Diagnosing preschoolers and children in middle childhood with low attention spans, emotional dysregulation, and the inability to self-control is rigid. After all, they are just kids, and these are a part of their personalities.

A busy child who is always in a rush and doesn't seem too fond of following rules can be just a regular, active child without being diagnosed. Some children have more energy than others, making them hyperactive. Nevertheless, they tend to calm down significantly over time as they mature and grow up, in most cases. So the real question remains: Does your child have ADHD, or is she or he simply a hyper, overactive kid?

What Does ADHD Mean?

This is one of the most common childhood neurobehavioral conditions (Ponnou et al., 2022). It is neither dangerous nor rare and is certainly not a disease. A disease is distinct and measurable, whereas a disorder does not have enough clinical evidence for diagnosis, according to Martin (2022).

It's a group of symptoms that may be seen in as many as 9.8% of the young population (3-17 years old), about 6 million in the

Chapter 1

United States of America, according to the last National 2016-2019 Parent Survey. ADHD is relatively hard to diagnose because the variety of symptoms can overlap with other disorders, such as autism, depression, anxiety, and sleep problems (Wright, 2022). Still, we will talk more about these in Chapter 7.

Some "core" symptoms include inattentiveness, hyperactivity, impulsive behavior, and restlessness. In addition, this disorder indicates that a child's brain functions differently from neurotypical individuals. For example, their frontal lobe is underdeveloped and lacks dopamine and norepinephrine (Chen et al., 2023), but we will get to that later. It also means it is challenging to recognize this disorder based solely on how a child acts.

What Does ADHD Look Like?
Many children may seem impulsive and act without consideration. Young boys are typically diagnosed and treated for being more disruptive and inattentive compared to young girls (Slobodin et al., 2019). However, these are not the only indications. Before we detail the different types of this disorder, I will cite a few symptoms that might sound familiar to you.

1. Have Trouble Focusing
Whether at school, daycare, or home, you can't expect toddlers or young children to stay 100% focused at all times. These kids will make careless mistakes and ignore close details.

It's not that they don't want to stay focused; they try but fail at it most of the time. They have a more challenging time focusing on anything longer than a few minutes than other neurotypical children.

2. Have a Low Attention Span
Just like they can't focus on one particular thing for more than a few minutes, they also have a noticeably low attention span. They may stop listening mid-sentence, and you'll probably find them staring out the window, scribbling and doodling on their notebooks, scratching their desks, or daydreaming.

3. Have Trouble Sitting Still

They tend to fidget and squirm when sitting and moving around. Their brain constantly forces them to make small movements with their bodies. You can also see them blinking their eyes unnecessarily, tapping fingernails, shifting their weight now and then, crossing and uncrossing their arms and legs, and other similar movements that parents usually reprimand children about.

4. Need to Move Around Constantly

Just like they cannot focus on one particular thing, you'll also find that these kids feel the need to move around almost all the time. Instead of staying in one place or sitting down, they will always prefer to move around, walk or even run when there is no need.

5. Talk Excessively and Interrupt Others

When something interests or fascinates them, they will find it almost impossible to stop talking about it, even when the listener is aware. These individuals can't comprehend that it is impolite to interrupt others when they are talking. They will interrupt you in mid-sentence, often with something completely unrelated. It's important to note that their actions are not intentional or intended to be rude. Instead, they are impulsive and can't seem to control themselves.

6. Will Fail to Finish Activities, Chores, and Work

Their limited attention span often leads to difficulties in completing tasks successfully. So, whether homework, playtime, chores, or any other activity around the house, you'll likely find them leaving the tasks incomplete and finding something else to do. Their brains are designed to always look for "something new" and "something more interesting," which propels them to leave what they should be doing.

7. Make Careless Mistakes and Forget Things

I am pretty sure you are beginning to see a pattern here. With a low attention span and a tendency to be easily distracted, these brains are also prone to make careless mistakes in their work and be consistently forgetful. For instance, these kids often forget the location of their belongings within a few minutes or misplace them because they struggle to remember where things should be stored.

8. Are Unable to Follow Instructions

Because these children can't concentrate on something long, they tend to "tune out" when receiving instructions. The result? Incomplete information to carry on an education wholly and correctly. At the same time, they are being distracted by something that's marginally more instruction because that's a part of their nature. So, when a teacher gives instructions, try as they might, an ADHD child will only receive bits of it and act accordingly. They will often hear only the first or last part of any instruction rather than the whole thing because they will most likely get distracted.

9. Have Trouble with Efficient Time Management

Most people with this disorder will have trouble with efficiently managing their time. In other words, **time does not exist!** If you tell an ADHD kiddo to finish their task "right then," they are likelier to complete it on time. On the other hand, if you give them work to "complete later when it is convenient," they will forget about it until it is too late. Why does this happen?

ADHD is more about the present and not the future. Therefore, they want to respect your instructions as long as their unique brain doesn't interfere. With thousands of stimuli to pay attention to, they need help creating space for something that needs to be done later.

10. Are Always Losing their Things

An annoying habit that often carries into adulthood. Having this brain is almost like going on autopilot! Your kid puts something down, but their brain is immediately distracted. They think of something completely different while their hands are busy with that action. Their physical activity is not even getting half the attention; hence, they will completely forget what they had done the next minute. So, which of these looks familiar to you?

What is the *DSM*?

The *DSM* is the *Diagnostic and Statistical Manual of Mental Disorders*. The name might be unfamiliar to parents or teachers. Still, the *DSM* is the reference guidebook published by The American Psychiatric Association (APA) used by healthcare professionals, physicians, and doctors in the U.S. and can be used worldwide. This is an essential guide for mental health providers.

> "This manual is a valuable resource for psychiatrists, other physicians and health professionals, including psychologists, counselors, nurses, and occupational and rehabilitation therapists, as well as social workers and forensic and legal specialists and researchers to diagnose and classify mental disorders with concise and explicit criteria intended to facilitate an objective assessment of symptom presentations in a variety of clinical settings."
>
> — THE AMERICAN PSYCHIATRIC ASSOCIATION, 2022

The *DSM-5 TR* is very detailed and technical, containing all the symptoms, descriptions, causes, and treatments required to deal with most mental health and brain-related conditions and disorders that children and adults can suffer from.

According to APA, it does not substitute the work done by a qualified mental health provider. This guideline also includes information on ADHD and acts as a Universal language. The latest edition of this book, the *DSM-5-TR* (TR meaning Text Revision), was printed in March 2022 and is available for purchase online. *[This suggested reading should be simply for research purposes.]* Written by professionals, this book also contains information on more than three hundred mental disorders and illnesses.

Why is the DSM-5 so important?

It is written, edited, reviewed, and published by The American Psychiatric Association (APA, 2022), with more than two hundred mental healthcare experts worldwide. The DSM-5-TR is the latest

Chapter 1

and most comprehensive version, encompassing vital insights into ADHD. This guideline holds significant value, serving multiple roles. When assessing potential mental health concerns in your child and seeking expert validation, the DSM-5-TR becomes a reference for diagnosis. Furthermore, it serves as the cornerstone for professionals to maintain current knowledge of mental disorders. Therefore, any emerging advancements pertaining to ADHD or other conditions find representation within this guideline, ensuring your healthcare provider remains well-informed. Based on your child's symptoms, mental experts can determine their criteria, which is extremely helpful when deciding on treatment.

Did you know?

A 2022 article by Mia Vieyra, an American clinical psychologist with expertise in ADHD who has worked in Paris since 1992 in private practices and a member of AAWE - (The Association of American Women in Europe), states that French educational systems consider and treat all children equally with great pride, which can be very challenging for a child with a mental disorder, whereas in the U.S. classrooms, there are more allowances for ADHD children to get up from their seats more often, have some "fidgeting materials," and have less homework or exercises than a neurotypical to show more comprehension (Vieyra, 2022).

They also have minimal options as prescription stimulants, with only methylphenidate available, also known as *Concerta, Ritalin*, and *Equasym*. (Ponnou et al., 2022). We will talk more about medication and stimulants in Chapter 6.

"In my professional experience, French teachers have come up with great plans for ADHD children and have very effectively implemented them; however, some do not consider this their role. On a positive note, I have found that for a subset of children with ADHD, the increased structure, stringent rules, and high expectations in a French classroom are actually very beneficial and provide them with much-needed and clear limits and boundaries."

— MIA VIEYRA, 2022

So it is worth knowing that teachers are trying to give extra help to children with ADHD in the classrooms. Unfortunately, it is rare in the French educational system.

Is ADHD a Modern Problem?
Not really. It's also true that in some countries, the modern world has only started to talk about it in the 21st century. For example, in the U.S., it has been extensively studied over the past 50 years (Faraone et al., 2003). This is a disorder that might have been in existence thousands of years ago! Astonishingly, the symptoms of ADHD were first noticed and mentioned in a book by Hippocrates, whom we know as the father of modern medicine.

Hippocrates lived in Greece in about 460-375 BC when he talked about a patient who "couldn't stay focused on something for long" - which we now know as one of the most essential and primary symptoms of this disorder according to Children and Adults with Attention-Deficit/Hyperactivity Disorder (CHADD, 2018). Hippocrates thought this loss of focus was caused by - in his own words, an "overbalance of fire over water." His suggestions? A diet of bland food, including fish instead of meat, plenty of fluid, and physical exercise (CHADD, 2018).

Later, around 1798, a Scottish physician named Sir Alexander Crichton also mentioned ADHD in a book he wrote. He termed it "the disease of attention," which is pretty accurate. He was the first to observe how people with this "disease" were always restless and had trouble focusing on one particular task (CHADD, 2018).

Physician and renowned philosopher John Locke discovered the same symptoms in a group of students who also had trouble paying attention to one thing for a long time (CHADD, 2018). So, as history tells us, ADHD is not a new problem in children or adults. It has existed for hundreds and thousands of years, though we have recently started to study it.

Chapter 1

What are the Different Types of ADHD?

ADHD is a behavior disorder, and since everyone is unique, it makes their condition different. This particular disorder is usually first discovered during childhood. At the same time, some symptoms are utterly contradictory to the most prominent ones. As a result, it can be categorized into different types based on a particular child's symptoms.

The information below regarding the different types of this condition is according to the *DSM-5TR Diagnostic Criteria for ADHD*. This mental condition can be of three major types:

- Inattentive and/or Distractible type
- Impulsive and/or Hyperactive type
- Combined type

All three of these criteria come with very distinct symptoms, which physicians use to determine the type of ADHD dominant in children. According to the Centers for Disease Control and Prevention (CDC, 2022), the symptoms may sometimes overlap, but only the most dominant ones are considered to decide a type.

1. Inattentive/Distractible Type

The symptoms of this particular category are what we most commonly assume in an ADHD child: having a low attention span and/or getting distracted easily. However, other more precise symptoms include:

- Poor listening skills, i.e., they often fail to pay attention to anyone talking to them, giving lessons, or giving instructions.
- Tendency to lose or misplace everyday items.
- Constantly getting sidetracked by external stimulation that's not very important at that moment.
- Forgetting to complete daily tasks like brushing teeth or changing clothes.

- Avoid tasks that are not too fond of or require attention for a long time.
- Regularly missing deadlines because of ineffective time management.
- They are often having trouble staying organized.
- Notable lack of ability to complete assignments or homework on time.
- Making careless mistakes at school or work because of inability to concentrate properly.

2. Hyperactive/Impulsive Type ADHD

This particular type refers to children always being on the go—signs of being extraordinarily impulsive and active. The symptoms include:

- Squirming and fidgeting in their seats whenever they sit down.
- Possessing lots of physical energy.
- Running, standing up, walking, or climbing during inappropriate moments.
- Being completely unable to play or engage in any activity quietly for more than a few minutes.
- Interrupting others when they are talking.
- Talking continuously on a topic that interests them without regard for the listener.
- Blurting out answers or opinions impulsively before the question is even completed.
- Being unable to wait their turn for something.
- Always acting impulsively without thinking about the consequences.

These symptoms can result in significant complications in a child's life, particularly at school or in social interactions, as they hinder their regular interactions with other neurotypical children. This can lead to them being labeled "selfish" or "weird."

3. Combined Type ADHD

The most common one is ADHD-C (CDC, 2022). It incorporates symptoms of impulsivity/hyperactivity and inattention/distractibility with varying degrees of severity. Having this classification doesn't mean your child's symptoms are more or less severe. I was diagnosed with combined type and some of my symptoms were so contradictory that no one knew what to make of me.

How is ADHD Diagnosed?

So should you assume your child has ADHD just because they seem distracted lately? Because they seem too eager to run around, always on the move, constantly climbing and jumping? Do they talk a lot and interrupt you when you are trying to explain something? This might mean your child is exactly what they are: children.

These are things that kids typically do at a certain age. For example, when we were young, we were all restless and chatty and looked for the chance to run away and join the circus! Therefore, the best course of action is to have them diagnosed by an expert.

It's a process with several steps. There is no single test to diagnose this disorder; instead, it can be misdiagnosed for other conditions because of similar symptoms. One measure of the process might also involve a medical exam, including hearing and vision tests, to rule out other potential problems (Seay et al., 2023). Let me tell you how your physician is going to examine your child. First, you must understand that some factors must be considered for this diagnosis. For example,

Number of Symptoms:

According to DSM-5-TR, children 4 to 16 must show at least 6 out of 9 symptoms listed in the DSM-5-TR with apparent severity to be officially diagnosed.

Who and where:

A psychiatrist, a neurologist, a psychologist, a certified mental health professional, or a pediatrician must be the ones to make the diagnosis.

Effect and Consequences:

The symptoms must negatively affect the developmental level in more than two settings, such as school and home, for at least 6 months and experience the symptoms before age twelve. What does this mean, do you ask? It means that if they are constantly distracted in class and missing out on their lectures, it may be considered a symptom of ADHD. On the other hand, if they sometimes seem to be daydreaming but not regularly enough in a way that affects them negatively, academically or socially, for the past 6 months, then it might be just something children do at times and won't be considered as a symptom in the DSM-5TR criteria.

Age Limit:

According to the DSM-5TR, for young adults over 17, at least 5 symptoms should be present for the person to be considered ADHD, but in reality, many clinicians "bend" the criteria when it comes to age. Some adolescents can get diagnosed with just four symptoms if they show significant impairment says Brown (2023).

Classification:

Remember that everybody can have difficulty sitting still, paying attention, or occasionally controlling impulsive behavior. For some people, the problems are so pervasive and persistent that they interfere with other aspects of their life: home, academics, social, and work life for adults.

Types of Testing:

How do you think the expert will test your child? Ask questions and tick them off? Actually, it's going to be more complicated than that. When an expert diagnoses your child, they will look at their entire life. They can interview family members, friends, teachers, and anyone affiliated with your child. It's a process that can take hours and several appointments (Seay et al., 2023). Also, having a teacher's report is essential because a one-paragraph can give a broader range of input than just a checklist (Hallowell, 2023). The doctor will consider the child's environmental factors and physical examination, such as skin, heart, neurologic system, and motor coordination.

In a 2023 article, Seay et al. state, *"Any good ADHD diagnosis will*

Chapter 1

begin with a clinical interview to gather the patient's medical history. This is often supplemented with neuropsychological testing, which offers greater insight into strengths and weaknesses, and helps identify comorbid conditions."

Computer programs and brain scans can be used depending on the doctor, but they can be expensive, and according to most experts, the most reliable process is found in the patient's history (Seay et al., 2023). Dr. Hallowell (2023) states, *"Scans are not a cost-effective way of spending your healthcare money, and they don't contribute much to the diagnosis of ADHD. But it seems that patients love seeing a picture of their brain, and the scans can often help them own the diagnosis."* In addition, The American Academy of Child and Adolescent Psychiatry (AACAP) also noted that these types of brain scans shouldn't be executed because they expose patients to high levels of radiation and don't give clinically helpful information (Mercuri et al., 2011).

Are ADD and ADHD Different?

Anderson (2023) states that ADD, or Attention-deficit disorder, is an outdated interpretation of ADHD. On the flip side, non-professionals who still use the term ADD out of familiarity usually refer to the inattentive type, such as poor focus, listening, and organization skills (Russo, 2023). The former term ADD without hyperactivity, as stated in the DSM-3 published in 1980 by APA. For example, Adler (2022) claims, *"We call all attention-deficit disorders ADHD."*

Can Signs and Symptoms of ADHD Be Severe?

Although ADHD is a common childhood behavioral disorder, it has a presence of 7% among adults worldwide, and 40-50% of children, once diagnosed, will still experience symptoms into adulthood (Ginapp et at., 2022). It was in the *DSM-5* that the severity levels were introduced, designating the levels as **mild**, **moderate**, or **severe** (CHADD, 2019). That is where the concept of the spectrum comes in!

Based on these criteria, experts now diagnose a child's type of

ADHD and determine their severity. This condition exists within the spectrum, where two factors are considered: their symptoms and intensity (DSM-5-TR, 2022).

- **Mild:** Few symptoms above the required number for diagnosis exist and affect two or more settings (home or school).
- **Moderate:** Symptoms between "mild" and "severe" are present.
- **Severe:** Many symptoms are present above the number required to diagnose and affect more than two settings in severe conditions.

Depending on how early the individual is diagnosed and the treatment progress, they may worsen or get more acute with time. It is worth mentioning that the severity established by the mental health provider does not reflect in a child's or adult's experience because it can change over time depending on the circumstances (Clarke, 2022).

[Remember, even when severe, having this condition is not the end of the world. We are lucky to live in a time when the severest of ADHD can be treated. I am an example of this, which I will explain in detail in the next chapter.]

What Causes ADHD?

Unfortunately, scientists have yet to determine the exact cause behind ADHD, so there is no specific answer. Nevertheless, recent research (Faraone et al., 2021) shows that **genetic link plays an important role.** It can run in the family as it did for my brother and me.

According to CDC, **birth factors cannot be ignored.** For example, children born prematurely or with low birth weight exposed to pesticides or lead are at risk of developing this condition in early childhood. Some scientists have also believed that **excessive stress or smoking during pregnancy can lead a child**

Chapter 1

to show symptoms of ADHD (CDC, 2022), but that theory has not been confirmed.

Problematic parenting, watching too much television, consuming too much sugar, living through family stress, and having traumatic experiences as a child - all these external factors might not cause ADHD. Still, they are responsible for worsening the symptoms (CDC, 2022).

As you can see, no exact reason a child might develop this condition exists. It can be one specific cause or dozens of small factors. It is something to understand, acknowledge and accept rather than something to analyze and dissect.

If your little one has this condition, they were born this way. Yes, some factors can interfere with symptoms, but overall you need to understand **that you can not change how their brain works** for the sake of the relationship between you and your child. Instead, **you must work with their brain and understand the best methods to support them with everyday obstacles.**

Now that we have reached the informative end of this chapter, I trust that you have acquired valuable knowledge about this disorder. Whether this has been your first book on this disorder or your 5th, I believe information is power, and you can never have too much of it. In the following chapters, I will drive straight to how you can help your child, which is the primary purpose of this book.

"It is better to be high-spirited even though one makes more mistakes, than to be narrow-minded and all too prudent."

— *VINCENT VAN GOGH.*

2
UNDERSTANDING THE SUPERPOWER

So, your child has been diagnosed with ADHD. You are anxious, hopeful, and fearful at the same time. You think of all the years they would struggle with their symptoms. It's okay. As a parent, you are destined to worry about your child's future. But this is nothing to worry about. Not so much, at least.

Having ADHD doesn't mean your child can't live to their full potential. In fact, it can be to be just the opposite. It doesn't mean your child is lacking. It means they have an untapped, raw, and brilliant SUPERPOWER. I am not being incredulous here. Nor am I making up stuff to make you feel good about the situation. I am only writing what I think is the truth, what I believe in.

... and what I have seen happen in my own life.

Understanding ADHD

Some analogies I believe can help you understand a bit more of what it feels like to have a brain like ours:

- Driving a car with squared wheels.
- Having many tabs open on an internet browser where they each play different songs, but it is impossible to find where the music is coming from to stop them.

- Trying to find the right TV channel for your favorite show, but you need help remembering which one it is, and someone else has the remote.

I can continue, but I believe you understand my point. For something more relevant, let's think of your child's disorder as participating in a three-legged race for the first time, which is an analogy I once heard from Tamara Rosier, Ph.D., the author of *Your Brain Is Not Broken (2021)*.

All your life, you have walked on two legs. But now, you must learn how to manage this new scenario where you have a third leg to control. Having an extra limb doesn't make the journey easier but more challenging. That's only because you have yet to learn the game's rules. When you understand how to utilize this "extra limb" you have given, you'll instinctively know how to use it best. You'll get ahead in the race in no time, before anyone else, because you have understood the dynamics of the race and the advantageous position you have been given.

So, like any other child, I, too, was weary at first of my limitations. I soon realized that I don't have a *deficit of attention;* just like the "extra limb" in the race, I have too much attention and don't know how to control it. That, my dear reader, is the beauty of ADHD. **Your child is not "lacking ." Instead, they have something extra that needs to be controlled and refocused.**

Do you like Superhero movies? I am crazy about them! In my favorite Superhero and science fiction movies, the young and powerful protege always needs the help of a wise and experienced mentor to control their power. Think of my experience as the qualification I need to become your child's mentor in this. Their Professor X. Their Jedi Master Yoda.

I am sure you are familiar with the Incredible Hulk, where we can associate Dr. Robert Bruce, the physicist's alter Hulk (the green-skinned, angry monster with outrageous physical strength), with ADHD symptoms.

So Dr. Robert would turn into the Hulk against his will when emotionally stressed. At first, he didn't know how to control his anger; he would destroy everything around him and hurt the people he loved. We see numerous failed attempts to control his alter ego, with him being aware of his acts when he was transformed into the Hulk. However, he was still very persistent in adapting and controlling his anger, using his great strength to help people instead of hurting them. This is something you can associate with your child's future greatest weapon.

Many symptoms of this disorder will discourage you, your child, and the people around you. Sometimes, you may have tried everything to improve it but failed. I know for a fact that with persistence, power of will, faith, discipline, patience, consistency, and much love, your child can achieve so many great things with this condition. This is a SUPERPOWER, not a limitation! All they need is to be in control of their ADHD so they can self-regulate, focus on what they choose to focus on and thrive, succeeding in their careers and their lives. Trust me as I help you to understand this condition better.

The Importance of Acceptance

What is the best way to show your child how much you support them? Love them? Yes, of course! No matter what, and even if! Shower them with gifts? No, that is not what they need from you. Ignore their symptoms and pretend like nothing is different. Definitely not! What your child needs the most from you, more than anything else, is this: ACCEPTANCE.

I grew up in a culture where it is entirely okay to yell at your children; even eventually, slaps were a common scenario in my memory. Of course, we weren't really hit unless we had done something heinous, but they were a normal part of our upbringing. Only when my family moved to the U.S. I noticed that physical punishment was unacceptable. It was a shock because I couldn't imagine a childhood without being hit by my parents, just as my new friends couldn't believe our upbringing.

I understand now that physical punishment is not good parenting practice, and they do more harm than good to children.

Chapter 2

I can't blame my mother because it was what she was taught and endured in her childhood. Hitting your child is not just a common practice in Brazil or South America; it is highly encouraged to keep children obedient and "on track."

My mother was, and still is, a very emotional woman. I remember how she would cry at any scene on TV, when sad music was playing, or even at any emotional advertisement. When she would yell at us or hit us, we could still feel the sadness behind her actions, which encouraged us to improve. She worked at two jobs all day, cared for her family, and even helped us with our worst symptoms, and for everything she - and my father - has done for us, we would forever be grateful.

You might question me: *If she loved you this much, why did she hit you?* It's difficult to understand our upbringing in a culture where physical discipline is unacceptable. Nevertheless, as I said before, it is more expected in my culture. Most of my friends also experienced the same thing, and we never thought to question it or stop it from happening. I'm not saying that hitting your child is okay! But in my culture, parents grew up knowing that hitting their children will make them obey the next time to be successful in life.

Thankfully, my brother and I didn't suffer any long-term consequences of physical punishment; instead, we became responsible and functioning adults when we grew up. We were hit when we did something terrible, but our parents also accepted our limitations and symptoms and did their best to help us. On the other hand, my friends were not that lucky. I have seen my closest friends getting yelled at for the simplest of reasons. Of course, this was done to discipline them, but all that mental and physical abuse eventually turned my friends against their families.

Before we were diagnosed, life had been difficult at home and school. After we were diagnosed officially by a professional, it surely didn't get easier. Still, my parents felt relief because it confirmed what they had always believed: *that we meant well, but our brains did not cooperate with the tasks and chores we had to do.* Did they have more patience with us because of it? Maybe 10 to 20%

more, which, many times, is still not enough. Though, they did try, and I know they did their best. Let me share a little anecdote here.

Another friend of mine showed similar symptoms when we were in school, a boy named Pedro who lived in our neighborhood. Pedro couldn't sit still in class for more than a few seconds. He rarely listened to what the teachers were saying; he stood up in the middle of the lesson to walk around, disturbing the whole class and frustrating the teachers. He had all the signs of having Hyperactive/Impulsive type ADHD.

After my brother and I were diagnosed, the school authorities advised his parents to do the same with him, but they refused flatly. They were aware of all his symptoms but chose to ignore them. Instead of accepting that their son had a behavioral disorder that needed treatment, they labeled his symptoms "impertinence," "rudeness," "disrespect," and "disobedience."

The teachers themselves were stunned at this attitude. Despite their insistence, Pedro's parents denied the possibility of ADHD. Instead, they believed it to be a made-up disorder that their son was fabricating, which is truly disheartening. They openly reprimanded their son, resorted to name-calling, and even threatened to have him expelled from school if he didn't improve his behavior.

The last I knew, some of his more severe symptoms persisted today, creating serious problems in his life, and it was all because his parents couldn't accept him the way he was. I could overcome my symptoms because my parents not only accepted my disorder but helped me through them; Pedro couldn't because his parents failed to do so. So I could feel his pain and, at the same time, appreciate what my parents were doing for me.

I appreciate my parents more and more every day for giving me a better childhood. More than anything, accepting your child and their symptoms is the best way for you to deal with their condition. In this perplexing state, your child wants your love and support; but more than that, they want you to accept them just as they are so they can learn to take their own shortcomings.

Understanding Your Child's ADHD Brain

Chapter 2

Imagine you are in a meeting, an interview, or a lecture. Whatever the person in front of you is saying is important to you. So you tell yourself to listen to their words. You acknowledge them and what they are saying and prepare your responses. You make that meeting/interview/lecture successful because you train yourself to remember the moment.

Other thoughts might come into your head if you are not listening 100% or the topic is not so significant to you, but you can force them out because you have that control over your brain. Most people can filter out the unnecessary from the necessary and control their focus unless they are extremely tired or ill.

For a child with ADHD, that filter is not there. Not just because they are children but because they are different and can't control their brains to obey. They know what is important to focus on at that particular moment, but they can't filter out the dozens of other thoughts coming their way.

So what happens to your child's brain when they know they are supposed to listen to the teacher? If your child is anything like what I was, millions of things! While the teacher's message holds significant importance, so does the distant melody of a singing bird, the gentle sunlight streaming through the windows, the rhythmic ticking of the clock on the wall, or the sight of a leisurely sleeping dog outside. Every single stimulus entering their mind has equal importance to their brain, making it almost impossible to focus on one. **Our brain gets bored easily and constantly seeks stimulation** (something more fun and exciting).

There is no such thing as time. If you tell a neurotypical child, *"We have to leave in 10 minutes,"* they are likely to time it in their head and know more or less how long they need to be ready to leave. For a kid with this disorder, it will unfortunately not work this way. It will sound like another language to them.

I still struggle with time, and everyone within the spectrum will as well until they understand the best method of not being late for something, such as different alarms, countdowns, or *Alexa* reminders. For example, I often think I have enough time to attend a meeting if I have 30 minutes. Still, I forget to consider the time it will take me to finish getting ready, drive in traffic, and potentially miss an exit because *Google Maps* can sometimes be confusing, and I end up being late...

They will have a **tough time accepting criticism.** When these kids face criticism, they often internalize it, perceiving their actions as consistently wrong and believing that they can never succeed again. Consequently, they may also suffer from varying degrees of depression due to the sense of rejection. Nevertheless, it is important to note that when someone provides them with honest feedback, it is genuinely motivated by care and a desire to witness the child thrive.

They often know what to do, but they do not do it. ADHD has nothing to do with unintelligence. In fact, they are pretty intelligent. The issue is in accomplishing the task they know they have to do. **Because of their impulsivity, they can't think twice or even think once before doing something.** Let's say the child is between three to 5 years old with ADHD. They will have trouble sticking with games and playing with their peers. They might snatch other children's toys, break them with no bad intention, or disrupt others. In the ages 6 to 12, these kids will have trouble complying with the classroom expectations and often draw negative attention, but with **no bad intentions.** Can you imagine what that is like for them?

It is tough for a neurotypical brain to understand an ADHD one. These children aim to avoid disrupting the classroom, causing frustration to teachers and family, or coming across as rude by attentively paying attention, refraining from interrupting, and actively collaborating with others. That is how these brains function pretty much all the time. Exhausting, don't you think? It can be excruciating for young kids to bear this on their own, having to conform to societal standards. Your acceptance of their situation is exactly what they need to flourish.

The 30% Rule

It is a rule of thumb that Dr. Russel A. Barkley mentions often, and it is a practical way to understand how parents and caregivers need to deal with a kid with this disorder. "*An average ADHD child is 30% behind their age*". So if a child is 10, they have the self-control of a 7-year-old, and **they need support corresponding to their executive age**, which in this case is 7. This means you must lower your expectations of them. Otherwise, this will be a very long and demanding "battle" where you always expect this child to behave and self-regulate to an age that is not equivalent to their executive age. You would ask for the impossible. In addition, Dr. Barkley claims it is the same for adults, so a 25-year-old has an executive function of a 17-year-old. Thinking of that made it more evident to me why it is harder for us to cope with some of the core symptoms of ADHD.

We will talk more about how to deal with this issue, but basically, what needs to be done is this: You need to re-arrange the environment around this child to allow them to show what they know. In the ideal world, they need support from you, your family, teachers, and school principals. People often disagree with acknowledging this disorder and are unwilling to help, which is the cruel and natural world. I have seen it and lived it through with my own life.

A Little Empathy Can Go a Long Way

We are genetically designed to feel empathy for a child. So when a child cries for a real reason, we instinctively feel compassionate for them, even when they are strangers. That is how compassion works for human beings. Though, what happens when you get called to school for the fifth time a month because your kiddo has disrupted the class or hit a colleague? When, despite reminding them repeatedly, your kid has forgotten to hand in their assignment at school?

What happens when your little one does not understand where they have gone wrong and/or why you are frustrated? Alternatively, they do understand but can't help avoiding doing the same thing again. What do you feel when others complain of your child being rude and disrespectful? As much as you love your kid, you would not feel very empathetic about them at that point when they show zero remorse. Even when you know it is their brain that makes them behave this way, compassion can be hard to muster.

It is easy to feel frustrated, scream at them for 'not trying hard enough,' or lose patience. Unfortunately, it's also the easiest thing in the world not to *feel empathy for them* because, let's be honest, there is a limit to a parent's patience. Compassion needs to come from the inside, and it is hard to do so when your child shows no signs of remorse or guilt. Just like they need your love and acceptance, they will thrive on your empathy.

Empathy is a complex emotion. It comes from the deep-rooted desire to help someone and relieve their suffering. In a way, showing empathy is better than loving your child unconditionally. How? Because when you are showing empathy, you are reacting to your child in a way that they feel loved, valued, heard, and understood. Your empathy will say that you want to help them because you recognize what they are going through and why they behave the way they are. It's telling them, "I understand, and I want to help." That is all your child wants from you. Do you want your beloved little one to cultivate this SUPERPOWER? Show them empathy when they are going through some very intense emotions.

Trust the Power of the Mind

ADHD is not a disease and certainly not something to despair of. Most importantly, having these symptoms doesn't mean some won't eventually go away. Physicians are efficient people. They will instead end their diagnosis without sounding very hopeful about it, mainly because they don't want us to get our hopes high. I have read a few books written by experienced doctors that don't sound very positive.

That is also one of the reasons behind my writing this book. I wanted to talk about ADHD in a positive manner so you know there is hope at the end of the tunnel. Doctors can be wrong, too.

How often have doctors predicted that a patient won't wake up from the coma, only to be proved wrong? How often have we seen

Chapter 2

them telling a patient they might not be able to walk again but witnessed a miracle?

These are not just miracles in movies but in real life too. So don't let anyone tell you that your child might never excel in school because of their symptoms or that they would have trouble succeeding in life! Disheartening is unnecessary even when their symptoms are severe and likely to continue into adulthood.

[There is a movie I recently watched and absolutely loved titled "The Dawn Wall ." I highly recommend it if you have not watched it. It is not related to ADHD, but I found it very inspiring.]

Based on a true story, "The Dawn Wall" is about how two world-famous mountaineers, Tommy Caldwell and Kevin Jorgeson, climbed the "unscalable" wall of El Capitan of California. Their journey, to be honest about it, was excruciating and dangerous. The El Capitan is known to be one of the most formidable rock mountains, and these two climbers showed immeasurable patience to climb the completely polished sheet of rock. It was not just a movie that was exciting and thrilling; what inspired me was how adamant these two climbers were in their plans.

What do you think these men faced when planning to scale the El Capitan? Encouragement or discouragement? Don't you think they were showered with "it's impossible" and "you'd never be able to do it" from the very beginning? How many people, do you think, told them to be scared and retreat? How many times did they doubt themselves? Did they listen to all the negativity? No, they did not, and that is why they succeeded.

Spoiler Alert! Don't read this next two {paragraphs} if you plan to watch the movie.

{The craziest part of this movie, in my opinion, was that Tommy climbed this impossible wall after having an accident with a woodcutter and ended up cutting off his index finger. Doctors told him they couldn't put the finger back with surgery and told Tommy he couldn't climb again like he used to because the index finger has 25% of the grip strength in our hands. Can you imagine the hardship? He climbed the unclimbable wall without his index finger, which can be considered unthinkable. It was not just the pinkie finger of his hand or a missing tip, but an entire finger, one of his most important ones, needed to pull his body up and grab things.

That is the **power of will**. Only possible when you have persistence and discipline. He had to go through many training hours to get where he was. He must have lost focus in the middle, doubted himself, and felt pain, blisters, and bleeding fingers, but it did not make him quit. Indeed he didn't feel motivated at times as we all do. He pushed through all the limitations and the impossible through discipline! Which I think is the most beautiful part of the movie.}

If you think about it, dealing with this disorder is a similar battle you and your child must face. Within the societal context of my upbringing, youths with this medical condition had to face something similar. People didn't believe us when we described our symptoms; most of the time, they thought we were only making excuses. It was hard for our parents not to be disheartened by everything they had to face.

Many of us exert considerable effort trying to control our symptoms through sheer willpower. However, much like other aspects of life, addressing your child's ADHD requires unwavering determination. This mental health condition is usually diagnosed when individuals are young, i.e., when they are 4 or 5. That is actually too early for a child to understand how their willpower can be used to fight the symptoms.

So it's your role to guide them - the parent, the guardian, the teacher, the well-wisher, and the best friend. Therefore, they must accept their brains before anything else. Acceptance doesn't mean we like or agree with something, but it's a step to improve ourselves. Our mind power is the strongest and the most adamant tool, even when your child doesn't know it yet. This power is theirs to harness, and I will teach you how to do so.

We have all heard that we can choose our own thoughts; they can affect our mindset and reality. I have always thought that was a bunch of nonsensical jargon until I practiced it myself. Every single moment of our lives, we have dozens of different thoughts competing for space in our minds, but not all of them are equal. Some thoughts are more dominant, and they are the ones that influence our future actions, reactions, and reality. So what do we do? We choose the thoughts we want to focus on. Not just the ones that are more dominant than others, but the ones we think will have a more positive effect on our lives, and you do this for your children.

You'll also see your kid's situation positively when you train your mind to focus only on positive thoughts. This will, in a significant way, change your attitude towards them, which they will also be able to feel. Without saying anything specific, controlling your thoughts will help you accept and acknowledge your child's condition in a better way. I am not just reaching out for the moon here. It really works, trust me! Let me give you an example.

If your young one has been diagnosed, there are many symptoms you have to deal with. If their childhood is anything like mine, there might be many complaints coming your way. My parents had also been through the same, and it was definitely not easy for them to deal with it all. While my father handled the situation better, my mother used to get stressed about it. She also had to think about our livelihood because Brazil was going through a bad economy then, which has unfortunately been worsening like the rest of the world. The stress brought out much negativity inside her.

It was a breaking point in our lives. My mother was stressed and worried, bringing out her worst side. She sometimes yelled and screamed at or even hit us, just like many children we know were treated. Nevertheless, she was trying her best, focused on and changed her thoughts.

Instead of focusing on the dozens of thoughts that screamed, "your sons are not going to succeed in life" and "your lives are ruined as you'll be stuck with two children unfit for society," she listened to the more positive ones. A few little positive whispers were inside her mind into her dominant thoughts. For example, she listened to the thought that whispered, "your sons are not lazy or disobedient. They are getting through this".

She let that one tiny whisper drive away all the negative ones in her head until it was the only thought that remained. It took a lot of patience and willpower, but my mother finally - after the initial shock of our diagnosis wore off - became the parent we needed to get through our ADHD. That, my dear reader, is the power of the mind that helped her look at the situation's positive side. I am thankful my mother shared this story with me. Trust your willpower and mind; you can help your child by choosing the proper thought to follow.

Do not Make Assumptions

This disorder comes with a list of symptoms, but there is one thing I would like to request of all parents: *don't make assumptions about your child.* All three types of ADHD have their own symptoms but vary from person to person. Assuming anything just because it says so somewhere could be one of the worst ways to deal with the situation. There are some kinds of assumptions that you definitely shouldn't be making, like:

♣ *"Children can only have a particular set of symptoms of ADHD."*
Wrong! There are different types, but the symptoms do overlap. That is what happens to a child with a combined type (Clarke, 2022). Example: me. Just because a child is inattentive in class does not mean they can't be hyperactive, either. There are absolutely no assumptions to be made regarding the symptoms of this disorder because they can be varied and contradictory.

♣ *"Everything will get better when they are older."*
This is another ultimately dangerous assumption. Yes, in most children, some symptoms lessen as they reach adulthood with the proper treatment, but it is not a given. For many individuals, this disorder is a lifelong condition depending on its severity, and some symptoms may linger well into adulthood (Tartakovsky, 2021). So, if you avoid dealing with the symptoms thinking they will eventually go away, it is not a safe assumption.

♣ *"We shouldn't tell other people about my child's condition."*
Wrong again. If no one knows about your kid's condition, they will quickly judge and label them as "lazy" or "disobedient." So it's not safe to assume that hiding the symptoms will protect your children because it will do just the opposite. Instead, if people know why your child is acting their way, they might make allowances and help them.

♣ *"ADHD will make my child more creative."*
It can benefit a more creative mind. Successful people with ADHD are entrepreneurs, inventors, the CEOs. It also depends on the person and is not something guaranteed. However, multiple studies by H. White (2006, 2011, 2016, and 2018) have shown that people with this disorder can be more creative than neurotypical individuals.

We are the outside-the-box thinkers; it depends on the parent's allowance and support of the child's creativity, letting them ask questions and express themselves, not saying "*no*" to their creative ideas even if they sound silly. The more "*no*" and "don't *do this*" they hear, the less courage to try again they will have; maybe at that very moment, it was not appropriate, but you know them the most, and keeping the children operating at the genius level is the best you can do for them to be creative.

Some very brilliant minds can be suppressed by their parents, guardians, teachers, or school systems by telling them to grow up, stop with the curious questions, and just do what they are told. Instead, let that inner child thrive by having them ask questions and support their ideas. My brother and I were very blessed because our parents mentally supported us.

♣ *"If they can focus on what they love, they can focus on what they're supposed to."*
I wish that were true! However, you see, one reason these kids can't focus on schoolwork or lectures is that these are things they might not be interested in. Unlike neurotypical individuals, who can control their attention span more easily, their attention wanders off to what interests them, sometimes not even so. This is one of the reasons these children stare out the window when the

teacher is lecturing in class because whatever is outside the window is more attractive to them.

One of the main problems of ADHD is not that these individuals cannot concentrate on anything; instead, they cannot control their attention.

❖ *"All children get distracted sometimes. It's not a disorder."*

Yes, and no. Most children are distracted when they are young, and if you think about it, it might seem they all have symptoms of this condition. Some of their symptoms are so severe and prominent that it affects them negatively academically and at home that they need treatment (Rowe, 2021). In addition, if left untreated, the symptoms might worsen over time. It's easy to close our eyes and hope their symptoms will gradually disappear on their own, but that's not the case.

Let Go of Perfectionism

Some of us are perfectionists; that is a unique way our brains work, where everything needs to be as perfect as possible. Tell them to make an omelet, and they will ensure it is a perfect circle. ADHD individuals, on the other hand, can be thought of as just the opposite. They usually race through everything, desperate to finish without thinking about the details or the best ways to complete something if it is outside their interest. Of course, the rule has some exceptions. Let me give you a small example from my childhood.

Instead of taking the time to carefully write down every word in my homework at school, as most of my classmates would do, I would rush it through. The result would be chaos. It was also one of the most common complaints my parents faced from my teachers. Although my work was passable, my presentation could have been better because I couldn't concentrate for long.

This is a massive problem. As much as they try to, they can't wait to make their work perfect, preferring to rush through it to finish it as soon as possible. So if your kid doesn't belong to that unique category of individuals who care about perfectionism, it's important to let go of those expectations. Forcing them to be perfect will only increase their anxiety and overwhelm them.

What you'll also need further is this: *a book where you'll learn how to be the parent your child needs you to be.* Other parents can help you with this, but so will this book.

"ADHD is a neurological and behavioral disorder that affects not only the person with it, but the entire family, including parents and the extended family of parental siblings and grandparents. It tests the limits of the family's ability to be supportive, understanding and loving."

— DRESHER LARRY

3
IT ALL STARTS WITH THE PARENTS

Till now, I have only scratched the surface of what it is to be the parent of an ADHD kid. The previous chapter was about acknowledging and coming to terms with your child's condition. From now on, it will be about how you can help them with their symptoms. Let's get down to business.

Parenting an ADHD Child vs. Parenting a Neurotypical Child

I believe in the power of mindfulness. It means that parenting for you will not mean just gliding through the motions but a continuous task requiring constant attention. For some people, parenting means feeding and clothing their children and seeing that they are happy and healthy.

After reaching a certain age, neurotypical individuals will take care of the rest as long as they are supplied with the basic necessities of life. Parents can cease to worry about their children after they become responsible enough to make good choices. Raising a neurodivergent child, unfortunately, can be twice or thrice as hard as raising a neurotypical one.

When you have a child who shows signs of ADHD, you'll have to give them more time and effort. Always. Similar to their

Chapter 3

newborn and toddler days, they will require your undivided attention. Yet, if you are also a working parent, you'll need more time and energy for it. I can say this because I have seen it happen to my mother. With two part-time jobs as a teacher and as a pedagog, as well as two ADHD children, she drowned in responsibilities and stress. Even with my father helping her, my mother faced a few turbulent years after our first diagnosis.

What other neurotypical individuals our age were capable of, we couldn't handle. So my mom and my dad, were in charge of everything: *our entire schooling, checking for our homework, ensuring we finished everything on time, helping us with our lessons, making us keep our rooms tidy and our chores completed.* They had to work twice as hard because neither my brother nor I could handle them effectively. It almost broke them until they gathered themselves up and learned to be their best selves.

This chapter revolves around how I witnessed my parents going through personal changes and transformations to become better parents for us, as well as personal experience from discussing with many psychiatrists and watching lectures with some well-respected pediatricians and general practitioners.

Become a SUPER-PARENT

Your child has a SUPERPOWER. So how do you respond to it? By becoming a SUPER-PARENT yourself. I am not asking you to be the perfect parent possible; I am not asking you to put unreasonable expectations on yourself to do everything perfectly.

Being a SUPER-PARENT has nothing to do with drowning your young one in luxury or ensuring they have everything they ask for. Your actions and reactions will shape your child's future and eventually make them the person they are destined to be. So how do you become the SUPER-PARENT so your child can have a good and long life? It will sound simpler than it is. You become the best version of yourself.

Do you think kids want a rich, successful parent who can afford everything they want in life? No! They want someone happy to care for them. Being content and fulfilled parent your child requires is the primary goal, with everything else being an added bonus. Be a parent who takes care of themselves. Be a parent who genuinely loves to be with their kids, and you can be a SUPER-PARENT, despite everything else in your life.

Make a Good Life for Yourself

A happy parent is a parent who takes care of themselves and their family. Mothers and fathers worldwide sacrifice a considerable part of their lives because they must care for others. Career, household chores, responsibilities of the children - everything becomes too much for a person to handle even when they have support. There are different ideas of a healthy lifestyle depending on where you live in the world, your culture, your financial situation, and your responsibilities. However, some self-care habits in life are universal and for everyone. Here is a brief list of everything that should be a top priority in a parent's life.

♣ *Eat Healthily*

Parents need to eat just as well as a growing child, if not more. In most cultures, like my own, mothers tend to sacrifice their nutrition for their kids. Especially in a financially struggling households, parents sacrifice a lot so the children can eat better. To be sure, I will cite a few things just so we are clear about what healthy food means because many times we grow up in a culture where some dishes are so popular, and we eat so much of them, we think that just because it is popular, it is healthy.

A healthy diet consists of the right amount of calories for our activity. Overall, have very colorful meals, so you consume lots of vegetables and fruits and cut down on saturated fat and added sugar products. Also, avoid excessive fried food; oil is a saturated fat high in calories, so you add calories and fat by frying any food. Depending on how long you fry a vegetable, you also lose its nutritional value. We will talk more about nutrition in Chapter 8.

♣ *Make time for Yourself*

I can't stress the importance of this tip enough. It's true you'll have a lot more responsibilities around the house, but that does not excuse you from making time for yourself. Whatever you want to do by yourself, for yourself, and with yourself, you need to make some time for them. You deserve a break more than anyone else in the world. So do whatever makes you happy and relaxed because you'll need that to face your responsibilities.

♣ *Compliment Yourself*

You'll be your child's model; they must see you admirably. Only you can do this for them by complimenting yourself as much as is natural. Find things in yourself that you think are positive and want to see in them, and congratulate yourself. Despite any weakness, your child needs to know that you see yourself positively. Trust me on this!

♣ *Never Think of Yourself as a Bad Parent*

You are already halfway there if you are trying to be a good parent! So never, under any circumstances, think of yourself as anything but a good parent. Indeed, parents can get angry at times and may resort to yelling, screaming, and saying things they later regret. That is because they are also human beings who have their limits and can sometimes get frustrated.

♣ *Ask for Help*

There is no shame in asking for help. Share your responsibilities with your partner at home, and don't stop accepting use from people who offer. Other people around you love your kids, and they would love to help, so always ask.

I have seen this in my mother's case. Being a proud woman, she would not share her troubles with others or ask for help. It ultimately caused her to feel more stressed when she tried to do everything herself. I recommend against this, not if you want to burn out.

♣ *Don't Blame Anyone for this*

It's not your fault they have this condition, and it is certainly not theirs. The best you can do is to work through the symptoms, support and help them improve over time. Playing the blame game, either on yourself or them - your luck or sins - is not going to help anyone.

♣ Focus on the Positive

No matter how dark everything looks, something has to be positive. Positive energy will always attract positive energy, and negative energy will attract negativity. So, we must avoid any negative thoughts as much as we can. Use fewer negative words and avoid gossiping or talking badly about someone. Children will pick up on that. There will always be something good and positive in your life that you can focus on instead of the negatives.

♣ Take a Vacation from Your Child

They need you, but you must also take breaks from them. It could be a few hours, a day, or even a week that you spend by yourself so you can focus on your life for a change. Some people would consider it a sign of bad parenting to want to stay away from your children, but just like people need a few days off from work, you also need some time off from your personal life. Whether you spend it in leisure or being productive, these days away from your kids should be a part of your life. It depends on many things; one of your main concerns should be to improve the quality of your own life. Only then you can give your child the patience and support they need to overcome this disorder. Take it from someone who has suffered because of this!

Stop Yelling and Start Connecting

My mother had always been the yelling kind. It took her - and us - some time to understand that yelling at children was not mentally healthy parenting. In fact, it made the distance between us more prominent. Because we were more likely to get yelled at, my brother and I gradually stopped sharing with her. For example, we would not tell her if we faced any new problems at school or even when anyone was bullying us. We would especially not tell her when our symptoms were taking over our lives and being too difficult for us to handle.

Because we were sure we would be yelled at, we stopped

Chapter 3

letting Mom help us sometimes. It turned out to be damaging in many ways. She got frustrated with our refusal to communicate and our secretive nature. Don't get me wrong. My mom was a fun woman when in a good mood. She is the best mother I have known in my life. She would only get angry and yell at us when stressed, but could have worked more against this stress and anger.

We learned something fundamental from this part of our childhood: *yelling is never a good solution.* It may feel like there is no way to make children listen without yelling, but this is not a healthy choice for parenting, at least not if you want a peaceful environment at home. It may also be because they might listen to your words but have difficulty processing them. In addition, these neurodiverse kids process information differently than others; thus, it might take them several tries even to understand the instructions. Do parents have that kind of patience? Not usually. When parents have to repeat the exact instructions a few times, they inevitably start to yell. It is natural but also one of the worst ways to communicate with them. Here is why.

With neurotypical kids, yelling at them is one way to get their attention and to make them listen. It may sound frustrating, but some children only consider it serious when their parents are yelling to do (or not do) something. Most children with this condition show signs of **emotional hypersensitivity** (Moukhtarian et al., 2018). Raised voices, yelling, and physical punishment can lead to emotional hurt, guaranteeing failure to discipline. In short, you CAN NOT yell at an ADHD child and expect them to obey. It simply doesn't work that way. So what do you do when you want your kiddo to listen? *You don't yell. You connect with them.* Here are some ways to approach these children instead of getting vocal.

♣ *Make them Say It.*

Instead of going ballistic for something they did or forgot to do, ask them calmly: *"Do you realize what you did wrong here?"* or *"What do you think you should have done?"* Be patient until they are the ones to realize what went wrong. If you constantly yell, it will only aggravate your child more. They will feel the need to be against you, no matter the situation. They will most likely yell back even when they know they are in the wrong. Instead, what you'll need to do is to make them realize the problem so that they can rectify it.

❖ *Know Your Child's Limitations.*

Stop and consider the situation from their point of view. Maybe they are not responding - not because they are not giving you enough importance - but because they need time to comprehend your instructions. Parents tend to get angry when children don't respond to their instructions the first few times.

What if your kid didn't understand that instruction? It would be unfair to start yelling at them just because they take longer to do something other neurotypical children can do faster. So, try to understand your child's particular limitations and take your time. Without getting angry or raising your voice, repeat the exact instructions as calmly as possible if they need you to.

❖ *Walk Away From it all.*

Is it an emergency? Is it something you need your kid to do at that very moment? If it is not, let it rest. For example, if your child is not responding to your instructions, maybe their brain is not ready yet. If this is something that can wait for ten more minutes and you find yourself getting angry with them, walk away. Come back after a few minutes when you have calmed down, and your child might be ready to listen to you so that you don't immediately start yelling at them.

❖ *Ask Someone Else to Take Over.*

So you keep telling your kid that playtime is over and they must put away their toys, only to meet complete silence. Either they don't hear you, or they are deliberately ignoring you. It is easy to get angry after repeating your instruction a few times, and now you get ready to start yelling. What do you do at that moment? If possible, ask someone else to take over the situation. Then, walk away and let another person continue: *a partner, a friend, a co-parent, or anyone you trust with your children.* This way, you calm yourself down before you start yelling and give your child a choice to respond better to someone else.

Do you like yelling at them? No, you don't. Does your child like it when you yell? Definitely not. Yelling is a big no-no when it comes to effective parenting. It's not just for your child's sake that you shouldn't yell, but for your own mental health too. Raising our voice to someone we love more than anyone else in this world can be emotionally draining for everyone. It's something to avoid.

For the kid soon to be a teenager, it's better to have an excellent controlled relationship with the parents. That is, by not just yelling and demanding them to follow the rules because they are good rules, but by giving them the option to express their opinion and input on these situations to create autonomy and build trust between children and parents.

Take a Deep Breath

Taking a deep breath before reacting in a potentially harmful way, such as yelling at a child, is a helpful and often overlooked tool in managing emotions and promoting calmness. It can give you a moment to pause and collect your thoughts before responding; it allows you to slow down and consider the situation more rationally rather than reacting impulsively based on emotions. Overall, taking a deep breath can be a simple yet effective way to manage emotions and respond more positively and constructively.

Know What Is Important for Your Child

There are two things youth need from us: *for you to love them unconditionally and also for you to discipline them when needed.* Yes, to love and discipline them may seem like two contradictory aspects of a relationship, but they must exist side by side.

Let's discuss the first aspect here: Loving your Kid, Unconditionally. This doesn't mean showering affection on them when they have been wrong or letting their misbehavior go unpunished. You can love your children and still be fair. Accept that their brains work differently and the extra work. Someone who will be distracted, act out, have meltdowns at inappropriate times, and need much reassurance. It would also mean loving someone who will need you the most in the world, more than anyone has ever needed you. Once you embrace those terms, accepting and different individual becomes more manageable.

Now comes the tricky part: Discipline Them.
It is hard to be strict with a child who is not intentionally misbehaving because they can't help it. Growing up in Brazil, part of our "discipline" was physical punishment by our parents whenever we did something wrong. It would have to be something very out of what was expected from us or something prohibited. As children, we did them anyway, and understandably, our parents got angry and frustrated at us.

While in our family, physical punishments were not used often, we got yelled at a lot; most of the time, it was from my mother rather than my father because he was calmer. Later, they realized that yelling - and hitting - have nothing to do with disciplining. It's true. Aggressive behavior, raising hands on a child, and even verbal abuse like yelling and cursing - leads to long-term mental health problems rather than correcting their behavior (Dorn, 2023). In addition, it hurts the family's relationship. There are better ways to discipline without leaving a negative mark on them. It's essential to be mindful of your actions, as they tend to become emotional about almost everything. Effective discipline necessitates skill, patience, and thoughtfulness.

Loving your kids and disciplining them are the same sides of the same coin. You can't choose one and ignore the other; they need to come together. If you only love your children and agree to their every whim, you'll spoil them forever. Kids spoiled by their parents, either with love or luxury, ultimately have a more challenging time succeeding by themselves.

What about only disciplining them without any trace of love in your behavior? That's actually worse. If the only thing your kid knows from you are harsh words and rules, they will have a hard time loving you. The love between children and parents is a beautiful and powerful emotion they will miss out on entirely.

Living a loveless life will take a toll on your children, and they will grow up cold, unfeeling, and emotionless. You might be able to scare your young kid into obeying you, but as soon as they grow up a little, they can easily discard you and your expectations of them. Love and discipline, therefore, go hand in hand. You must show that you love and can be strict with them.

Disciplining your ADHD Child

Parents are usually the first ones to notice that something is different or wrong with the child, which can lead to tension in the relationship. Because the child does not obey the rules, parents often feel they need to step up their discipline, being more demanding, controlling, and less empathic and patient, which is really sad. This principally happens with those using the "*old school*" parenting method, meaning all kids must follow the same rules with the same methods.

What would happen to a child if you started being tougher and more demanding? There will definitely be more fights and stress in the relationship, and the snowball effect will keep worsening. Instead of supporting and getting closer to the child, parents push them away, making it hard for them to cooperate. A huge part of disciplining your children is ensuring they behave in a way that's by your own rules and the rules of society. We know it is for their own good, even when we must be a little harsh with them every now and then.

Now, children have a completely different idea of what their life should be like. So, instinctively, they reject every bit of discipline coming their way. Thus, every interaction becomes a tug-of-war between these two parties. Of course, the easiest way for parents to get through to children who are not ready to listen is to raise their voices, hands, or both. Who has the energy or the time to approach every single argument with logic and patience?

Yelling the instructions at them should be enough, don't you think? Wrong! Every parent yells now and then, more out of frustration than anything else. Unfortunately, it helps us more than it helps the situation; we might feel better for the moment, but it does not mean our words are welcomed by our children.

When yelling is used as a disciplinary method, it loses all potency. These disciplinary methods will only hurt them and create an irremediable distance between you. There are better ways to discipline your child than raising your voice or hands.

♣ *Have Realistic Expectations*

First, you should lower your expectations depending on the situation. All parents hope to have the perfect kid who will never be in trouble and always cooperate, but the reality is quite different. At every stage, you must prepare to deal with what is natural for children: *crying, tantrums, lying, misbehaving, unreasonable demands, and nagging.*

You must modify your expectations to what is more fitting. Yes, they will need more work than a neurotypical child and will have trouble fitting in anywhere, so you must prepare yourself. Remember to use the 30% rule that we have talked about.

♣ *Set Your Limits*

Explain the limits before you yell at them for breaking them. They need to know the rules as much as possible. Every family will have a different set of rules. At the same time, be clear about the consequences of breaking the rules. These kids should know what punishment awaits them. Whether it's the loss of privileges or being grounded. They NEED to know where their limits lie and hear it repetitively for their brain to register it properly. Be clear when making these rules and keep your word.

♣ *Be Fair. Be Equal.*

Whatever set of rules you make for your home, they should always be the same. If your kid is allowed two hours of screen time daily, then so be it. If breakfast is a family affair, every single member of the family should be present in it. It doesn't matter if you have one neurodivergent child and one neurotypical, one school-going and one college-going; the rules should be (almost) the same for everyone. If, for any reason, the adults need to skip family time, explain it to the child as evenly as possible.

They should understand the reason behind breaking the rule instead of settling for "we're adults. We can do whatever we want." It helps an ADHD child register the rules better when they see them implemented on every family member rather than only on a few.

❖ Be Consistent

Sometimes parents give in and break their rules out of sheer exhaustion. It must be avoided, even when agreeing to anything, just for a few moments of peace. What is allowed in a household should always be allowed, and what is off-limits should always be so. If you are not committed to your own rules, your child will pick up on that and be tempted to test your limits further. It should be clearly mentioned beforehand if you allow special privileges for particular reasons - like birthdays or vacations.

❖ Be Appreciative of Good Behavior

To reinforce good behavior, you must show appreciation to them. Your child needs to know what they have done right and why it was right. So never stop saying, *"What a good boy/girl! You have cleared away all your toys without asking. Now I can relax and spend time with you because you have greatly helped me."*

It does not just help them feel good about themselves; it also gives them a good idea of the behavior expected from them. In many households, good behavior is taken for granted quietly, but bad behavior is pointed out. While this may seem practical, it could be more favorable to kids. Be appreciative, be encouraging, and you'll see a visible improvement in your child's actions.

❖ Initiate Positive Attention

Every young individual with this condition is a storehouse of energy that is very hard for a parent to follow through. They will seek you out with questions, comments, opinions, and insights. If they need more attention from you, they might even try a few misdemeanors. A great way to nip it in the bud is to initiate positive attention for them from your side, i.e., spend quality time with them. A 15-minute to 1-hour playtime every day with your child should be enough to assure them that you are giving them both time and attention.

✤ *Be Smart with your Instructions. Break it up*

They generally have trouble following a chain of command. For example, telling them *"change your clothes, wash your hand, comb your hair and come to dinner"* will only confuse them. A neurotypical individual might accomplish those commands, but an ADHD kid is likelier to lose track after changing their clothes.

Instead, follow single instructions: *"change your clothes."* Then: *"wash your hands" only* after they have completed the first instruction, and so on. It can take longer and a lot more patience, but it will get the job done, and if you follow a routine, they will eventually be able to pick up on your multiple commands.

Use a whiteboard to give instructions. Write down everything you want them to do on the board - responsibilities/chores they need to work on, with check marks on the things that have been done. **Use sticky notes** around the house. If children get visual instructions besides just hearing them, it will be easier to follow and remember.

✤ *Use Time-Outs*

They are a way to give your child time to calm down and get their brain less tangled up. If you don't phrase it well, time-outs will feel like punishment and they will definitely put up a fight. So instead of saying, *"Go to a corner and think about what you have done!"* try it this way: *"Why don't you go to your special corner and spend some time there until you are feeling better?"* This way, you are not punishing them; you are simply giving them some alone time so they can calm down their frustrated brain.

✤ *Pick Your Fights*

These kids will probably display attention-seeking behavior multiple times daily. They will mutter under their breath, whine, complain, make loud noises, bang on surfaces, interrupt you, and not cooperate when you need them to hurry or make faces at you because they are angry, frustrated, or want some attention. Finding the best parenting methods in your case will set them up for smoother navigation through life.

Chapter 3

. . .

Be a Fun Parent Who is Also a Friend

The parent's life is hectic and full of chores. We must complete hundreds of tasks from morning to night to ensure the kids are fed, clothed, safe, healthy, and happy. Where is the time to play with them? Where is the energy? With or without a career to worry about, a parent barely gets a moment to catch their breath.

The responsibility doubles up, along with the additional attention you have to give them. Over time, after a few years of following the same routine, day in and day out, parents become merely machines programmed to go through the motions. Despite that, when they are young, we are their world. Before school and friends, we are their best friends, playmates, and their companions in all things imaginary and creative.

Children require parents who can fulfill the role of caregivers and friends. However, these kids often struggle to make friends themselves. They rely on their parents more than anyone else, needing them to be more than just providers of meals and bedtime routines. Although it may seem ideal in theory, many lack the energy or time to engage in extended playtime with their children, especially if they are hyperactive. Nevertheless, there are ways to incorporate moments of fun and bonding into your life with your child.

♣ If you are a working parent and not the primary caretaker of your child, **plan a special time for you at least once a week**. It doesn't have to be long or something major, but maybe an ice cream run with just the two of you, a long drive on the weekend that's only about you two, or a movie night together in the safety of your home.

Whatever it is, big or small, it needs to be fun, just the two of you, and something your child looks forward to the rest of the week.

♣ **Introduce family game nights**, something for the whole family to enjoy. These don't have to be more than once or twice a week, or maybe even once every two weeks, but they should be something for everyone.

Work and gadgets should be entirely off the table when you are playing, and your total concentration should be on the game and with each other.

✣ **Find a hobby that you can enjoy together,** something that's quiet and preferably requires you to sit down together. It could be reading, painting, making crafts together, doing puzzles or building LEGOs, or anything that is age-appropriate, enjoyable, and invites much discussion.

✣ No matter how tired you are or what a bad day you have had, **never shy away from a few moments of goofy behavior with your child.** Something as simple as making faces to take selfies, running around the house, playing hide and seek, kicking a ball around the yard, or tickling each other silly only takes a few minutes every day, but they will give your child good memories for hours.

✣ **Never refrain from making silly jokes with your child or laughing at theirs.** Instead, make fun of yourself so they laugh and don't take it seriously when they are also making fun of you. Most children don't mean anything disrespectful by doing so; if your little one considers you as a friend, try to keep it light and funny between you.

✣ **Take an active interest in their friends, school, interests, and hobbies.** Include their friends in your outings sometimes if that is what they want. Make them understand that you want to be involved in their lives as a good friend would.

✣ **Do something physical together, such as ride a bicycle, go for a run, jog, or play a sport.** Any physical exercise makes a person happy, creating a bond between the two that is stronger and more durable.

You can spend little or much time being the fun parent. You must be involved in their lives in a way that's more than just disciplining or instructing them. Despite all their worries and chores, these kids deserve a parent who is fun to be around and genuinely wants to be involved in their lives.

The bottom line is: to show your kid that you enjoy spending time with them and that their condition doesn't stop you from having fun together. A child facing many problems at school needs a parent who is fun to be around at home, a parent who is also a friend to them. This is important because when hard times come, the child can trust their parents and not be afraid to share their feelings.

Shower them with Loving Touches.

It's true some children - especially ones in the autism spectrum - don't like to be touched. But most of these kids love to be hugged, kissed, and cuddled. Through physical touch, they seek comfort, assurance, and satisfaction. Even the most hyperactive child can visibly relax when they are hugged when feeling overwhelmed or frustrated.

What happens when you hug or touch your ADHD child? Physical touch is just as crucial as nutrition, sleep, and daily exercise. Young kids, in particular, initiate hugs, cuddles, and kisses every now and then because they want to feel assured and comforted, a characteristic that regrettably diminishes slowly as they age.

I remember my mother asked us not to stop calling them "*Papai*" and "*Mamãe*" - two words we used to call affectionately, which I believe you took a guess... They mean Papa and Mama. My mother's logic was simple: she did not want us to grow older and stop calling them the cute way because we would not be their child anymore but adolescents. Since she preferred us to use the terms of affection, we have used them ever since we learned to talk. I still call my mother "mamãe" because it makes her happy. It is just a little thing but a special bond between us.

All these symptoms can be tolerated when they are extremely young but can become frustrating and problematic as they age. What happens when children can't easily manage what they might see other friends deal with? Tantrums, meltdowns, crying, frustrated tears, and overwhelmed feelings. Words don't help at those times because they are most likely to fall on deaf ears. What help are reassuring touches, hugs, and even a hand on their back.

Any physical contact helps release some oxytocin, dopamine, and serotonin in your child's brain (Holland, 2018), which causes warm and fuzzy feelings in a person and lowers anxiety and stress. We sometimes call oxytocin the "love hormone" for this exact reason. It creates the feeling of being in love or "in bond" with someone, and you can do the same for your little one when the situation needs it.

A loving touch can mean many things to your kid when feeling overwhelmed or anxious. It will tell them you love them, assure them of your support in everything they can (or can't do), give them the courage to face something and help them calm down. The need to touch someone we trust is embedded deep into us; this is why we reach out for a hug after a bad day or why a baby calms down when held. We are all the same regarding being assured with a loving touch.

Not all families are used to getting or giving hugs. However, there is no need to worry. I will provide a few examples of situations where initiating some form of physical assurance will be helpful for your ADHD child.

♣ If any specific kind of social situation is difficult for your little one, i.e., going to school or meeting friends, **always give them a long hug before**. This and a few deep breaths will help them prepare for the next few hours. Sometimes, when these kids try to explain something but become too emotional about it, they have trouble finding the right voices. This happens especially when they are trying to tell you about something that has hurt them or the injustice they have suffered.

A long hug makes them calm down in such situations to explain better later.

♣ During a group discussion, some of these children have a hard time getting their opinions across or getting their voices heard. They might start to get agitated and anxious when this happens. **Please hug them or place a hand on their back and apply gentle pressure until they can calm down and try again.**

♣ These children also get angry very quickly and easily. It does not take them much to start screaming or throwing a tantrum, but you can bring the situation under control quickly.

Leave them alone if the temper is too much to handle; **hold them in a tight embrace after a while while they may sob, yell or even whine.** A hug in these situations can do more than a thousand words.

❖ Not just for diffusing certain situations, physical touches can be helpful when you want your child to pay attention to you.

For example, if you feel like they are not responding to your instruction, **get down to their level, turn off the tv or any other distractions, touch their arm or hold them by their shoulders, and then repeat your instructions.** They will remember your instructions (or your warnings) better this way.

❖ Another great way to calm your whimpering or whining child is to **use eye contact if possible, and touch coordination.** Hold them gently and then talk to them; they will calm down faster. I have known this technique to work in social situations if your ADHD child suddenly finds everything too overwhelming.

There is a misconception that when children are not looking at you when you are disciplining them, they are not listening or paying attention at all, where in reality, for some, it is easier to pay attention when they are looking into the distance, if you demand them to look into your eyes when giving orders they will be trying to focus on not losing eye contact rather than actually paying attention to what you are saying.

Apart from all these dire situations, it's always better to give your kid hugs and cuddles occasionally. If you are not a family that initiates these, it is time to start. Most children with this disorder find any kind of physical contact reassuring and comforting, and a huge part of parenting them would be to anticipate when they need a hug, a cuddle, or a pat on the shoulder.

It's good to start doing this as they are young so they understand the importance of affection and how love needs to make the world go around. I have met families where the dad does not hug or say "I love you" to his sons because they are uncomfortable with it. It lacks so many emotions that later can be trapped inside their hearts. Teach your children always to express themselves, but if you don't do it as a parent, more significant obstacles will have to be faced.

Be a Zen Parent.
Being Zen is something that belongs to more than just the *millennials* with their high-powered careers and busy social lives. Parents need this more than anyone else. Parents of young kids have the most hectic time ever. With part-time or full-time jobs (or even two jobs in some cases), a family, a home to look after, and multiple children, parents tend to be busy every single moment of their lives.

"Zen" is a relatively new concept for Western cultures, but it has been a part of Eastern philosophy for centuries (The Zen Studies Society). As I see it, being "Zen" means entering a state of complete calmness and attentiveness. However, this is a state you must enter automatically, by intuition rather than by meditation. With practice, diligence, patience, and learning to let go of what worries us the most, we can all become Zen over time.

Parents, in general, have a more challenging time with this realization. If you are like most parents in the world, you'll ultimately be unable to stop worrying about your children. No matter their age, you'll still be anxious about them, getting frustrated at their choices, or irritated at their behavior occasionally. While trying to live your own life, you'll also be responsible for theirs. If that doesn't sound like something to be anxious about, what does? Still, parents need to achieve some level of "Zen" in their lives. I don't know if you have heard this before. There is an excellent serenity prayer by an American theologian that I love:

> *"God, grant me the serenity to accept the things I can't change,*
> *courage to change the things I can,*
> *and wisdom to know the difference."*

— REINHOLD NIERHUBR

Doesn't that sound perfect? I wish it were that easy! There would be many things in your child's life that you would want to change but can't; all you can do is learn to accept them. Only then may you accept your child exactly as they are. In the previous chapter, I wrote about accepting your children's limitations and symptoms, but I will add more here. This time, I will give you a few mantras I need you to repeat to yourself every now and then, especially when your patience is challenged. This part of the book is more about accepting yourself as a parent than accepting your child, only through which you can achieve an actual "Zen" state. Repeat these mantras every day or as many times as you need to.

♣ **I am Not Alone in This.**

That's true. You are not alone in raising a child who has ADHD. Even if you don't see other parents around you with children facing similar difficulties, there will be others. Find those people in your locality or via the Internet, such as Facebook Groups, and you'll not feel alone again.

♣ **I don't have to be Perfect.**

Indeed, society expects parents to be perfect, but that is neither possible nor important. Your child does not need a perfect parent; they want someone who loves them no matter what. You can do that!

♣ **Parenthood is supposed to be enjoyable.**

Being a parent is this magnificent gift that life has given you. It comes with worries and anxiety, but having fun with your children is one of the best ways to spend time together, and you should definitely remember that.

♣ **Making painful decisions is a part of being a parent.**

Sometimes, you'll have to make heartbreaking decisions, but they must be done. Even if your child seems to hate you during these times, tell yourself you know you want the best for them.

♣ **It's not possible to always get it right.**

You must make essential decisions almost every hour. Not all of them will be correct, but that's okay. Just as we sometimes make wrong decisions for ourselves, we might make worse ones for our children. Forgive yourself if you have done so because it is impossible always to be right even when you have their best interest at heart.

♣ **This was always going to be complicated.**

Being a parent was always going to be complicated. Remember this when things get too rough, and you'll envision a better future for your family.

♣ **My life is a Marathon without any Breaks.**

Marathons do end, and it will be glorious when that happens. While the race is going on, your life will be a constant flurry of actions. You'll have to do everything you do to survive while running. It may seem like you are exhausted, but you only get to stop when the race ends because that is the most important thing: *you have to finish the race.*

♣ **My Sense of Humor is my Weapon of Choice.**

How are you going to face every hardship that comes your way? You can cry and whine about it or smile through it all. Learning to take everything lightly and with humor is one of the greatest gifts you can give yourself. It would not solve all your problems, but it would make it easier for you to deal with everything.

♣ **There is a lot to Celebrate in my Life.**

You don't always have to wait for significant achievements to celebrate your life. Yes, graduations and anniversaries are fabulous, but the little things are just as important. What seems like regular incidents in our lives are tremendous accomplishments for our children.

Learn to celebrate all the good things, such as good grades, that one time they remembered to hand in their homework in class or when they made a new friend at school.

♣ **I won't let Other Parents get me Down.**

While most people around you'll be supportive and helpful, you'll likely find some people who will make it hard for you to accept your child's disorder. For example, some "well-meaning" parents will ask why your 4-year-old is still writing their "Bs" and "Ds" backward when other children can do them correctly. You can get angry at them, get mad at your child, or get angry at your situation in life. Alternatively, you can ignore them and get on with your life. Also, learning to control your ego will help you greatly in this journey. It's your choice.

♣ **I won't compare my child with others.**

This is one of the worst things you can do, to compare their advancement in life with other neurotypical or neurodivergent children. It's not a matter of who is better or worse or even who is normal or not normal; your child is unique, and that is a fact.

♣ **I Trust my Instincts.**

When the child is yours, you need to trust your instincts. They will be your best guide in the challenging years to come. You might be wrong sometimes, but your instincts would be the best possible feeling to trust when making certain decisions for your family. Of course, everyone else in your life - well-meaning relatives, doctors, teachers, neighbors, and other parents - will have opinions.

♣ **I am not going to Lose Myself.**

You are a parent, but can't let that be your identity. Making time for yourself, your friends, your hobbies, and your career is still essential. Don't let your parenthood get 100% in the way of living your life.

♣ **It's Completely Okay to Take Help from Others.**

Just like you care for your children, you must let others care for you. Never shy away from accepting help when someone offers it, especially if it means you can take a break from parenthood. One mistake parents make is not to leave their child alone with someone else or send them to playdates or parties. If you trust the people offering, this is a chance that you can definitely take.

♣ **I Can Forgive Myself.**

Chances are, you'll make mistakes. you'll make bad decisions, and your children will resent you sometimes. You can't torture yourself forever for that; it won't right the wrong or help you make the right choices next time, but you'll need to forgive yourself for the mistake. Just because you are a parent, it does not mean you are not above mistakes or forgiveness.

♣ **I will Make time for my Relationship.**

Whether married or in a relationship, you must have a good and mentally healthy relationship with your partner to provide for your child/children. It will create a more pleasant and healthy environment for you and your family.

Cambridge Dictionary states the meaning of "Zen" this way: *"relaxed and not worrying about the things you can't change."* Your child's ADHD is something you can help with but not something you can change. You can't ignore the fact that they are having trouble adjusting at school or in social situations, but you can accept it. You can't change the fact that they are struggling with what other neurotypical children can easily accomplish.

What you can do is become a "Zen" parent who accepts the situation and is okay with what they can't change. So, repeat these 16 mantras above when the situation calls for it, and you can ultimately find the strength to be the parent your child needs you to be.

Set Out with a Mindful Approach

I don't know what you think about "mindfulness," but I swear by this approach. Many people I know have been known to improve significantly by practicing it. If you are entirely new to the idea, let me give you a small introduction to what "mindfulness" or "being mindful" is.

To *be mindful* means to give your full attention to something. Just like concentrating hard on something when engrossed in an exciting movie or book, mindfulness means slowing *down and paying attention to everything you do.* Mindfulness is the exact opposite of multitasking or automatically rushing through something. Let me give you an example. Take something we do every day, automatically and without thinking, like brushing our teeth.

Do we even break down every single action that goes into brushing our teeth every day? No. Since we do this at least twice daily, our hands, mouth, and body automatically go through the action while we are probably thinking about something else. What if we are mindful when doing this simple, everyday task?

Chapter 3

What if we turn brushing our teeth into a mindful exercise? Let me take you through the steps.

1. Before starting, relax your body.
2. Relax your neck and jaw.
3. Please take a few deep breaths and deliberately release them.
4. Take your toothbrush in your hand. Take a few seconds to think about how it feels in your grip: *Is it cold? Is it warm? Is it hard? What is the texture? What color is the toothbrush?*
5. Take a few seconds to think about what you are holding in your hands.
6. Take your toothpaste and gently unscrew the top.
7. Apply a small blob of toothpaste on your toothpaste.
8. The hint of the toothpaste should be prominent in your nose since you are concentrating hard on it. *How does it smell? Is it refreshing? Is it fruity or mint-flavored? Do you like it? Does the smell awaken something in you?*
9. Start brushing your teeth, minding each and every stroke. Think about what you are doing: *How does the toothpaste feel in your mouth? How does the toothbrush feel? Can you feel the bristles of the brush against your teeth? How does your gum or tongue feel? What does it taste like?*
10. Rinse your mouth with water and think about each step. *How does the water feel against your hands? Is it warm or cold? How does it feel when you are rinsing your mouth? Do you feel cleaner, fresher, and more awakened?*
11. Concentrate on your breath while you rinse your mouth, wash your face, and wipe your face with a towel. *How do you feel? How does your skin feel? Is the towel soft or scratchy? Is it warm or cold? What color is the towel?*
12. Feel gratitude for this simple task. Feel gratitude for your teeth and how the simple act of brushing makes

you more aware of everything else.

It might seem strange to you if you have never practiced mindfulness before. Trust me, try it once, and you'll feel a world of difference in your attitude toward life. It does not have to be about brushing your teeth, but any of the regular tasks that you usually go about without thinking:

- *Doing the dishes*
- *Drinking your first coffee of the day*
- *Chopping vegetables*
- *Walking*
- *Even relaxing at the end of a hard day*

I chose the action of brushing our teeth because this simple task - that we usually want to skip because it is too tedious and unexciting - can be converted into something soothing by changing your perspective about it. What is better is that by being mindful when brushing your teeth, you can set the tone for the rest of your day in the morning or use it to relax at night before you go to bed. Was I able to explain mindfulness adequately? I hope so. Now let's get down to mindful parenting.

You need to be the calm one. As much as you want to, you CAN NOT scream at them or lose your cool in any way. Unless you are the serene one in the situation, you can't expect your child to do the same. If you practice mindfulness at other times, you can connect to your agitated child in a manner that wouldn't have been possible otherwise. For example, when your child is overwhelmed, you can consider everything going on.

Mind your Own Bad Habits

We all have a few bad habits; that is a given. No one is 100% perfect, and as long as our negative practices are not harming anyone, they can be tolerated. What shouldn't happen, though, is to expose our children to our bad habits. Our habits will affect our

Chapter 3

children even when we consider them too naive or too young to understand.

Consciously or unconsciously, our children learn from us; the problem is that they don't learn from listening to us but by imitating us. We can keep telling them "not to lie" or to "share with friends," but they won't learn until they see us doing the same thing.

As we grow older, we acquire many habits that we don't think much about. For example, we lie to escape awkward situations; we cheat people thinking it is harmless fun. We are rude to people because we are in a hurry or having a bad day, and sometimes we might think it is okay not to share with other people who need something more. We do this in front of our kids, thinking nothing about our actions. Then we try to teach our kids good habits because that is expected of a decent human being. That is where we fail, because **WE PREACH WHAT WE DO NOT PRACTICE**.

I want to give an example here. Have you watched the American TV show, Modern Family? I am hoping yes because it is a fabulous show and extremely popular. This Tv series is one of my favorites, mainly because it is hilarious. I can't go through even one episode without laughing out loud. It is a delightful comedy about three modern families based in California, facing the ups and downs we all must go through in our lives.

One of the families is a gay couple, Mitch and Cam, with their adopted daughter Lily. In one of my favorite episodes, the parents start noticing that Lily dislikes sharing her things with anyone: toys, clothes, food, and books. They couldn't figure out why this happened and blamed her friends at school. Later in the episode, they are called to the school to discuss this situation. The school director complains about this habit: *Lily has difficulty sharing her things*. However, Mitch and Cam defend themselves and their daughter because they have always taught Lily to share.

Do you think maybe she is picking this habit up from her parents? the director asks because that's what kids do. They pick up good and bad habits from their parents and other family members. They then realized that Mitch, one of the fathers, also had trouble sharing. He would always have trouble sharing his belongings, even with his partner: his drinks, food, and clothes.

This embarrassed Mitch because they realized that telling *their child how to behave was not enough.* You need to show them how to. Children will pick up on our habits, so we must lead by example and act how we want our children to behave. They look up to their idols, and you have got to be the best version of their heroes. ADHD children need their parents to be true to their words because their brains react differently to lies and deception. So instead of learning what we tell them to learn, they do the opposite.

Kids with ADHD tend to lie more than neurotypical to escape undesirable tasks or cover their tracts. This is because they are more used to deceiving others based on their desire to avoid punishment and prefer to lie than to answer questions like "Why weren't you paying attention?" or "Why didn't you complete your work?"

These are habits that parents want to eliminate in their children, while we are doing the same ourselves all the time. Watching parents lie and cheat gives children a further "license" to lie and deceive themselves. To teach our children - especially neurodiverse ones - proper behavior, we must be mindful of ours. As adults, some of our bad habits might not seem harmful, but they can have a severe negative effect on our children, and that is definitely not something parents want.

Before you help your child, you must be the best version of yourself. This means to be your best self physically, mentally, emotionally, and spiritually. It is imperative for every parent in such a position to prioritize self-care, nurture their well-being, and develop the strength and capability necessary to be resilient caregivers.

"Behind every young child who believes in himself is a parent who believed first."

— MATTHEW JACOBSON

4

ADHD ISN'T A LIMITATION

The worst thing any parent or guardian can do in this situation is to consider it a limitation for their child. Far from it, this disorder might be your child's greatest weapon. I have said this once before, and I was not just being flippant or condescending. I do believe that a child's ADHD - even when it is severe and not likely to go away - makes them special and helps them to stand out from the rest of the crowd, making them unique.

Impulsiveness can sometimes be an issue, but it can also be a reason for them to **take more risks without fear or be more creative**. It's worth noting that we don't plan a time during the day when we get creative; an idea can come out of nowhere and will come out of **impulsivity**.

Distractibility is a significant factor in these neurodiverse brains and can get us into trouble. Still, on the other side of the coin, you get **the curiosity**, which makes us always want to know more, "what is this?" and "Why is that?" which is prior quality for innovators, for example.

Your child, and their brain, need the right kind of motivation to advance. However, you, the person so worried about them, also need to understand something: *ADHD is not a limitation that will stop your child from living their best life. We are the Outside of box thinkers!* At this moment, your child needs nothing more than your help and support.

Learn How Motivation Works For Your Child

"If you study hard now, you'll get good grades, and everyone will be so proud of you."

"You're such a good child to listen to your parents. Other children can learn so much from you!"

"If you're good, everyone will love you."

"If you do well in this test, you can have any toy you want."

These are just some ways people usually motivate a child to behave or pay attention in school. Nevertheless, neurotypical children are easier to motivate by promising them a reward, more affection or making an example out of them.

ADHD brains are not so easy to motivate. They don't have the motivation that comes within; they need the environment to encourage them, you, caregivers, family members, and teachers. So make deals with them, and explore the best solutions for your unique child.

There is one thing I have learned from my own experiences. It's not that these kids don't understand motivation. The problem is somewhere else. I have an analogy and would like to share it with you. Think of your child's goals as a recipe they must follow to make a dish perfectly. For example, if they want to make and eat waffles, they must know all the ingredients, their quantities, and when to add what. With neurotypical people, their goals come with immaculately written recipes they can follow. *"Add baking powder, and your waffles will rise." "A little sugar will give you that perfect sweetness."*

Motivation for neurotypical children follows this exact same technique. First, you tell them what to add and why. Then, they can follow the recipe while understanding why and what they will achieve. A neurotypical brain can improvise even if some basic ingredients are missing from the recipe. They can get over the missing information when they understand what their waffles will

Chapter 4

look, smell, and taste like. But what happens with ADHD brains? Why can't they follow the recipe? Because sadly, almost half of the recipe here is intelligible.

At the same time, this person has never even tried waffles before. So they need to find out what the finished recipe is supposed to look or taste like. Imagine you have just received your Grandma's old recipe book, but it's almost disappearing, and the names of some essential ingredients are gone. Can you make the same waffles from that recipe? Doesn't it seem impossible to you?

That is precisely how neurotypical and ADHD brains view their goals, but they have different perceptions and paths. For example, they both want to make amazing waffles. Still, they are stuck with different recipes: *one complete and detailed with explanations, and the other incomplete with missing ingredient names and vague descriptions.*

Doesn't that sound unfair? Is it fair if you applaud a neurotypical person when they finish making the waffles perfectly and call an ADHD person "lazy" and "unmotivated" because they couldn't? The thing is, a neurotypical person would not be able to see that half of the recipe is missing. *They can perfect the recipe with a few missing ingredient names, so why can't an ADHD person do the same?*

When this is the case, even a child with ADHD starts thinking the same way. They are frustrated and confused about *why they can't make something delicious with the recipe they have at hand when other people are doing the same.* Therefore you have to motivate them differently.

Motivate Your Child the Way They Understand It

The kind of motivation your kid needs is entirely different from what a neurotypical one is, and understanding that is a massive part of being a parent to a child with this disorder. Sometimes our brain has different motives and priorities than we do. First of all, you have to remember this: *your child will have trouble with tasks that are:*

-Lengthy

-Repetitive
-Boring

Sounds very familiar, doesn't it? Even neurotypical brains have trouble concentrating on something they don't like or what seems boring to them. At the same time, some things automatically stimulate them, and these happen to be things that are:

-New to them
-Urgent at the moment
-Of Personal interest

It's your job to find something that naturally motivates them and make everything else motivational. It's a tough one, indeed. Let me give you a few examples.

Make it Urgent:

Your child is due a science project; there is still a week to finish. Though, this kind of relaxed deadline does not help them. While neurotypical children might work better with an extended deadline, putting in a little work every day, an ADHD individual would most likely forget it or ignore it until the last moment. It's much better for these kids to create a sense of urgency. **It could be a false deadline** a few days earlier than the actual one.

You can implement the 10/3 minute rule. Do the homework for 10 minutes and take a break for 3 minutes. You can experiment and see what works for your kid. Don't make them do their homework right after school; they have been there all day, and they need a break, physical exercise, and playtime in the park to ease their brain for the homework.

Timers work great. In fact, this is a technique that I still use as an adult. I set up a timer for an hour or two in which I have to answer all my emails, get some work done or cook my meals, i.e., chores that I am not interested in doing.

Another technique that also helps to make a job seem urgent. This is by **setting up several smaller deadlines instead of just one final one and having to check up on each of them.** For example, when I have a few thousand words to write, I divide them into several deadlines and have my wife check on me with a

Chapter 4

"How far along are you?" or a *"How many words have you written down?"*

Having someone check up on my work boosts my productivity in completing tasks. You might want to spare your child the accountability you know they hate, insisting on completion or asking for updates. You might want to tell them to *"take your time, and get back to me whenever is convenient for you,"* but it does not help them.Instead, it creates a sense of urgency that will help your child complete something on time and do an excellent job

Make it Novel:

Now, it's not always possible to create something new and exciting for your child to do every day, but you can *make it seem fresh*. Whenever I find myself procrastinating work, I find new cages to work in. I order new and different tea flavors to help me feel the situation is new. I use a different font or even a new color. I buy new journals for myself to make notes on. So while the work is still the same, I find new environments and ways to do it. Let me tell you something: *It really helps me.*

If your kid doesn't seem too keen on finishing their homework, change the setting. Ask them to work in the garden, in the car, dining room, kitchen, or even in the garage. Buy them a new pencil, notebook, or anything else to help. Even when the task is something they must do every day, you can make it seem fresh to them.

Make it Of Personal Interest:

These kids have difficulty concentrating on something they are not interested in. Well, to be honest, don't we all? In some cases, they also have difficulty focusing on what interests them. Neurotypical children can be influenced to focus on activities they may not particularly enjoy, yet still perform well in those tasks.

So, what parents need to do is to make everything into what interests them. Let's start with something simple. When doing their lessons, **teach them examples related to their favorite cartoon, superhero, or book.** Go like this, *"If Batman saved 100 people and Superman saved 250 people, how many people did they save* *together?"* Not just that, but make it into a thrilling story so they can picture the lesson better.

Announce instant rewards. *"Do well in your studies, and we'll take you to Disney World next summer"* is not as stimulating as *"Finish this homework, and you'll get to watch TV for an hour,"* even though they are worlds apart. Long-term awards are too far to understand. **A verbal acknowledgment of** *"Good work,"* **a sticker, a raffle ticket, a star** - all work better for these children.

If possible, **allow them to engage in what interests them** rather than what you think is good for them. For example, you might think your kid needs to be more active, but they might be better interested in reading or crafting. Even if they flutter from hobby to hobby, the best way to keep them happy would be to let them do what they like with the proper guidance.

When your child has to work with a recipe missing more than half the necessary ingredients, there is no use reminding them *how important it's to complete the recipe* or *how urgent it's*. They already know all this and are stunned at being unable to complete it. Instead, try to see the missing ingredients in the recipe the way they see it and fill it up the best you can. Make the job seem new to them, make it seem urgent, and help them to find some personal interest in it.

Know how the ADHD Brain Works Scientifically

Until now, we have gathered much information about *how* an ADHD brain is different; it's time to know why it's different. I am not going to spend much time here, but I think it's essential for parents and guardians to know the scientific reason behind why our brain is as it is.

This disorder affects the brain, resulting in reduced volumes in five subcortical areas as well as an overall decrease in size. (Hoogman et al., 2017). The difference seems to lessen as the child matures into adulthood (Braaten et al., 2017). It does not mean these kids are not intelligent or sensible, but their brain affects some behaviors and thought patterns (Sinfield, 2022).

In an individual with ADHD, the brain's frontal lobe, amygdala, and hippocampus are smaller than in a neurotypical (Sinfield, 2022). Amygdala and hippocampus are responsible for emotional processing and impulsivity (Hoogman et al., 2017). The smaller prefrontal area affects their cognitive functions, such as concentration, impulse control, motor activity, memory, and inhibition (Sinfield, 2022).

If you want to look into more details, the neural pathways don't mature at the same rate as neurotypical brains and have a slower time connecting to each other (Sachdev, 2021). As a result, it makes it harder for these children to pay attention to what is right in front of them or focus on what they need. In addition, it can impair executive function, which means they also have trouble with organization and handling routine tasks (Sachdev, 2021).

Their brain chemistry is also different, as it releases less dopamine than the regular amount in a neurotypical individual (Sachdev, 2021). Dopamine is the hormone that regulates movement, sleep patterns, learning mechanisms, and attention—also known as the reward hormone (Sonne et al., 2022). As you can see, the brain's undeveloped frontal lobe and the chemistry make it much more difficult for an ADHD child to concentrate, regulate their movement, and learn what other neurotypical children their age learn quickly. Doesn't this help you understand their symptoms better now?

Plus, evidence from brain scan studies shows these differences between ADHD and neurotypical brains. So there is no reason for this stigma where uneducated people say it's a made-up condition... My brother and I grew up sometimes doubting whether we could overcome these symptoms in life, but our parents always reminded us how special we were.

She always told us we had a lot to offer to this world, which is the best approach you can take for your child. Instead of putting negativity into their heads, **praise their strengths.** You need to remind them how important they are and how important it is to keep trying to become the best version of themselves by accepting their brain.

. . .

Every little thing counts.

Another way I would like to think to treat ADHD is like the placebo effect. The placebo effect is triggered by the person's belief and not the actual impact of the pill. So if your child was diagnosed with this disorder, you need to make sure that inside their head, they know they will get better, and this is not affecting their future negatively because the placebo effect is nothing but the power of our mind. Professor Ted Kaptchuk of Harvard, whose research focuses on the placebo effect, says, *"The placebo effect is more than positive thinking — believing a treatment or procedure will work. It's about creating a stronger connection between the brain and body and how they work together."*

Know Other Brilliant ADHD Brains

To think that ADHD individuals won't succeed in life is entirely baseless. Please take a little break as I tell you their stories. The *"Outside of the Box Thinkers"*

❑ **Leonardo Da Vinci**

Do I have to tell you what kind of a genius this man was in every way possible? Can you imagine that he had ADHD? Da Vinci was a painter, sculptor, engineer, mathematician, scientist, and architect. His paintings - including the Mona Lisa, the Last Supper, and the Vitruvian Man - are human history's most remarkable art pieces.

Da Vinci was known to have many symptoms of ADHD and wildly chaotic organizational skills. He was also known to work on multiple projects simultaneously without completing them first. He had trouble completing most of his projects and was constantly on the move, always looking for something new to work on. Sounds familiar?

❑ **Albert Einstein**

Chapter 4

You might never believe it, but the world-renowned scientist Albert Einstein was a classic case of ADHD. Einstein, the most influential physicist of the 20th century, developed the theory of relativity, which changed the course of physics forever. Einstein was known to be extremely forgetful and quite unaware of his disheveled looks. He was also completely unaware of his surroundings and lived by his own rules.

☐ **John F. Kennedy**

Kennedy was the 35th President of the United States of America, but he also had countless other achievements in political and economic crises. As a student, however, he was mediocre and had trouble concentrating on his studies. He was not diagnosed with ADHD because it was not even considered a disorder until the 1980s. However, all his memoirs and stories about his childhood confirmed that he had many symptoms of ADHD and dyslexia.

☐ **Michael Phelps**

This Olympic gold medal winner and celebrity swimmer has faced multiple DUIs because he couldn't concentrate while driving. He even had to go to rehab a few times because he couldn't manage some of his symptoms.

Phelps was diagnosed with ADHD in sixth grade because his teachers noticed he couldn't stay still during class without fidgeting. It was also one of the reasons that he later got interested in swimming and could swim for up to three hours every day without getting bored or tired.

☐ **Bill Gates**

The co-founder of Microsoft Corporation, the chairperson for the Bill and Melinda Gates Foundation, computer programmer and entrepreneur Bill Gates himself admitted to struggling with ADHD all his life. According to him, he has always had trouble learning things or concentrating on one thing for a long time. His ADHD was one of the reasons that he dropped out of Harvard because he couldn't wait to finish his education before starting Microsoft Corporation.

☐ **Adam Levine**

The lead vocalist of the pop rock band Maroon 5 and famous

79

singer Adam Levine has also admitted to battling symptoms of ADHD all his life. Even as an adult, he has trouble writing down his lyrics on paper or during recording sessions. Levine was diagnosed with ADHD as a teenager, but most of his symptoms continued into adulthood. He still works with a doctor to manage his more severe symptoms and also helps a national education campaign to motivate youngsters with ADHD named "Own It."

☐ Jim Carrey

One of the funniest actors in Hollywood, Jim Carrey - known for his brilliant roles in movies like "Bruce Almighty," "The Mask," "Liar Liar" and "The Cable Guy" - has been battling symptoms of ADHD almost all his life. Nevertheless, according to him, he can't stop his hyperactive behavior, which, fortunately for him, has bettered his performance.

Carrey had always been upfront and honest about his ADHD to the media and even used his celebrity status to normalize it and educate his fans about it.

☐ Jamie Oliver

Award-winning celebrity chef Jamie Oliver is a British TV personality, author, and entrepreneur who reported his struggles with dyslexia and ADHD as a child. Because of his symptoms, he couldn't concentrate on his studies and instead focused on what he loved best: *the culinary arts.* Currently, he is a food activist and a chef, and he also advocates for global healthy eating to manage symptoms of ADHD in children and adults.

So you can see, if your child has been diagnosed and has many problems concentrating, self-regulating, and cooperating, there is no need to despair. Instead, you let them choose what they want to do with their life with the guidance you believe to be correct. After all, they are kids, and you need to support and guide them with their decisions, and one day, they will succeed.

> "Strength does not come from winning. Your struggles develop your strengths. When you go through hardships and decide not to surrender, that is strength."
>
> — GANDHI

5
TRAINING AND THERAPY

Brain training, behavior therapy, social skills training, "psychotherapy," "family therapy," and "parenting skills therapy" - these are some phrases you'll hear when you start treating your child's ADHD. Research by the Division of Developmental and Behavioral Pediatrics at Children's Hospital of Philadelphia in 2022 shows that many families of children with ADHD don't conduct evidence-based treatments. Therefore the results are insufficient (Nissley-Tsiopinis et al., 2022).

Apps on Brain Training for ADHD:
Brain training usually refers to a vast selection of programs, solutions, exercises, and tools designed to strengthen a child's brain. On that note, many studies on brain training were conducted, but not enough evidence was found on benefiting from this condition's symptoms (Michaels et al., 2022). Rabiner notes: *"It is important to examine the claims and evidence of specific applications. Making a general conclusion about brain training for ADHD is almost like making a general conclusion about medication for ADHD, where medication would include not just meds specifically developed for ADHD but a much wider range of medication."*

In other adequate studies, experts conclude that the person can improve their score on a working memory game, ability to read, or other measures of intelligence but not necessarily improve these abilities in day-to-day life (Michaels et al., 2022). An article entitled "*Brain Games Are Bogus*," published in 2013 in the New Yorker, states:

> *A pair of scientists in Europe recently gathered all of the best research — 23 investigations of memory training by teams around the world — and employed a standard statistical technique (called meta-analysis) to settle this controversial issue. The conclusion: the games may yield improvements in the narrow task being trained, but this does not transfer to broader skills like the ability to read or do arithmetic, or to other measures of intelligence. Playing the games makes you better at the games, in other words, but not at anything anyone might care about in real life.* - (Melby-Lervåg et al., 2013).

Most experts agree that further research is required to prove brain training efficiency with ADHD patients (Michaels et al., 2022). So be careful in researching ways to deal with these symptoms. Unfortunately, many of these brain training apps make claims that are not scientifically proven to work.

Types of Therapy

1. **Cognitive Behavior Therapy** is often combined with medication (Dodson, 2023). The therapist helps the child or parents become more aware of their thoughts, accept their feelings, and develop practical ways to strengthen positive behavior and reduce negative ones (Pedersen, 2021).
2. **Social Skills training/therapy** involves teaching children how to behave suitably in social scenarios and helping them understand societal norms, such as queuing, sharing toys, and coping with teasing (Pedersen, 2021).

3. **Parental training/therapy** is where parents are educated on various methods to positively comprehend their children and work collaboratively with them to manage organization, stress, and communication more effectively (Pedersen, 2021).
4. **Psychotherapy** is where older children talk about what bothers them and what struggles they have to face every day at school and home, and also learn how to best deal with them (Pedersen, 2021).
5. **The organizational skills training** goal is to develop concrete skills to help these children organize their things, books, clothes, accessories, and homework (Pedersen, 2021).
6. **ADHD Coaching** will consist of a few training types cited above. The professionally trained coach will help the diagnosed person organize their lives, such as time management, developing systems for success, healthy communications, strategic planning, emotional and intellectual growth, and other general social skills (NeuroHealth Associates, 2020).
7. **Neurofeedback** is a biofeedback therapy that uses real-time monitoring of brainwave activity to help individuals learn to regulate their brain function (Marzbani et al., 2016). During a neurofeedback session, electrodes are attached to the scalp to measure brainwave activity, which is then displayed on a computer screen. The individual then engages in activities, such as playing a video game or watching a movie, while receiving feedback on their brainwave patterns. This feedback is often of audio or visual cues, such as sounds or images, indicating when the brain produces the desired activity patterns. While neurofeedback has shown promise as a non-invasive and drug-free treatment option, it's still considered an alternative therapy. More research is needed to

understand its effectiveness and long-term benefits fully.
8. **Play Therapy** helps children with ADHD calm anxiety, improve self-esteem and provide reassurance. The therapist will watch and play with the child and reacts to the child's perspective. By playing with young children, they can feel connected and assure them of safety (NeuroHealth Associates, 2020).
9. **Music Therapy.** Listening to music, we like increases dopamine levels in the brain, according to a 2018 study published in the *Proceeding of the National Academy of Sciences.* Dopamine regulates attention, working memory, and motivation (NeuroHealth Associates, 2020).
10. **Art Therapy** helps neurodiverse children and adults express themselves visually by drawing or painting. It's highly effective for hyperactive children as it keeps their hands and triggers a level of focus not always achieved in talk therapy (NeuroHealth Associates, 2020).
11. **Equine Therapy.** Now, this is an interesting one, and reading all the research on the efficiency of this type of therapy made me think, why is this not talked about more often? This is a form of therapy incorporating horses. The client will partner with a horse for mental health treatment. The participant will groom, pet, feed, lead it to different locations and even bathe the horse! One thing they won't do is ride the horse, according to the Equine Assisted Growth and Learning Association (De Marco, 2017).

Equine therapists ensure it is safe for children to interact with horses (Arabi, 2022). Most of us have seen a horse close up in real life. They are majestic creatures. The therapists can also incorporate some CBT that allows the children to talk freely about their emotions arising from the horse's company (Arabi, 2022).

Overall many pets can have a significant impact on our mental health. For example, research shows that oxytocin (the love hormone) is released in the brain when interacting with dogs or a pet that you are close with (Marshall-Pescini et al., 2019). Although these therapy sessions mainly deal with talking to, discussing with, and understanding each other, they should still be presided over - like any professional therapy session - by a counselor, a therapist, an ADHD expert, or a pediatrician.

Behavioral Therapy

According to the American Academy of Pediatrics (AAP), behavior therapy is usually considered before medications for children diagnosed with ADHD under 6 years old. Despite that, for children 6 years and older, medication will be recommended with behavior therapy (E. White, 2021). *Behavior therapy* is an umbrella term, action-based, used to treat various mental disorders such as ADHD, depression, anxiety, eating disorders, and more (Cherry,2022). It helps to reinforce desirable behaviors with a reward system and change the unhealthy ones causing them distress (Gotter et al., 2022).

How? By either ignoring the negative behavior or taking away privileges, depending on the seriousness of it (Brown, 2013). In addition, behavioral training can involve their family and teachers working with the child to solve the current problems and monitor their progress (Pederson, 2021).

Different types of behavior therapy, according to the CDC, include

- Parent training in behavior management
- Behavioral Interventions in the Classroom
- Interventions with colleagues that focus on behavior
- Organizational skills training

Even the simplest everyday chores can feel challenging to these kids, they know what needs to be done but just can't do it. Yet, different behavioral therapy can help these children develop new, more positive behaviors, making their life more accessible

(Gotter et al., 2022). The best results for any child come together when everyone involved in the child's life comes as a team to help each other.

If you opt for behavior therapy without medication, you can expect up and down quality (Sprinkle, 2021). Your child managed to be at the breakfast table on time on Monday due to behavior therapy. It does not mean they will do the same on Tuesday. If that is the case, **praising their success on Monday is more important than arguing why they were late the day after.**

Cognitive Behavioral Therapy (CBT) is one of the most researched types of therapy, according to Cherry (2022), a Psychosocial Rehabilitation Specialist and educator, the different techniques of CBT are:

-Identifying Negative Thoughts
-Practicing New Skills
-Goal Setting
-Problem-Solving
-Self Monitoring

For progress to be made, the family members of the diagnosed child **must be willing to make changes.** Changes are often tricky, take small but definitive steps, and it will be worth it in the long run. Since the old methods led to a development problem, behavior therapy indicates that new methods can fix it (Cherry, 2022).

Now that you have an overview of the potential treatment plans, your child's pediatrician will consider their specific condition and the severity of symptoms to determine the most appropriate course of action.

Some Extra Tips:

1. Have your child **do things with their non-dominant hand.** So if they are right-handed, have them use their left hand to brush their teeth, use a fork, and open a jar. You can also make it fun by challenging them to do so.

This improves their motor coordination according to the study Chopsticks Manipulation Test (Park & Son, 2022). Though many people claim it makes them more intelligent by using the non-dominant hand, research does not indicate so, according to Benjamin Philip, a neuroscientist at Washington University (2019).

2. Take your child to **musical instrument lessons**, principally piano. Research by Dr. Ana Pinho in 2013 at the Royal College of Music in Stockholm shows that jazz pianists have an extremely efficient connection between the different parts of the frontal lobe compared to non-musicians. That is the area of most problems in an ADHD brain. It also improves brain integration (Hyde et al., 2009). My mom had my brother, and I took piano lessons when we were younger, significantly contributing to our executive functioning. I also recommend you talk to the teacher to have the child learn the songs they like because one significant discouragement was playing songs I had never heard before and did not like.

3. **Have your child improve their communication skills at family dinner time.** Share moments of your day that can be a lesson for them for the future, and ask them what challenges they faced on that day so that you keep them sharing their feelings and thoughts.

4. **Teach them how to juggle!** If you don't know it, try learning yourself, watch youtube videos, or get a friend to teach it. Let me tell you, it's so much fun. I recently started juggling three balls, and it's a fantastic feeling; the benefits are priceless. According to a study made at the University of Oxford by Johansen-Berg (2009), juggling enhances connections in the brain.

In addition, an article made by *Juggling Balls Australia* states that it also:
-Boosts brain development

TRAINING AND THERAPY

-Accelerates the growth of neural connections related to memory
-Improves hand-eye coordination
-Bi-manual dexterity
-Problem-solving
-Delayed gratification
-Body awareness
-Vision
-Improve academic skills as well as writing and reading

Because of the coordination you acquire after learning to juggle, your reflexes and coordination are also enhanced, making it easy to learn other skills. I wish I had started juggling earlier in my life. The cool thing is that juggling is egalitarian, which means a 9 year-old can be just as good as a 30-year-old.

With the infinite ways and tricks you can juggle, it will be hard for your child to get bored; always remember to cheer them up. Our brain is like a muscle; we need to train it. Why do you think athletes practice every day? Why do they wake up early before everyone else and practice? They are good at other games, but still, they train every day.

Anyone who wants to run the marathon practices every single day. Why do you think this is? Did they forget how to run overnight? No, they did not. However, athletes know the secret to success: *no matter where you are in life, how advanced or lacking, you need to train yourself constantly.*

That is where the notion of brain training comes in. Since your ADHD child has trouble with basic and everyday tasks, they must train their brains. Therefore, they must practice daily.

"This is a mental health issue not a behavior issue! People including doctors and schools need to recognize it as such!"
— Ridge Meadows

6
LET'S TALK ABOUT MEDICATION
MEDICATION DOES NOT CURE ADHD, BUT IT CAN HELP.

You can't expect any kind of medication to magically cure your child's symptoms or turn their brain into a neurotypical one. However, they can help with some of the most severe symptoms. Incorporating this chapter into my book presents a challenge since I lack the credentials of a medical professional or mental health specialist. Instead, I have grown up with ADHD and still struggle with many symptoms. At best, I can give parents and guardians many valuable tips on managing this disorder, but I can never prescribe any medication or recommend anything.

That responsibility will fall entirely on licensed physicians and experts. The NeuroHealth Associates (2020) states, "*The research is clear: ADHD medication paired with behavioral therapy is the most effective treatment for attention deficit hyperactivity disorder (ADHD) in children — particularly those who also exhibit oppositional behavior.*"

A 2010 Boston Massachusetts General Hospital study found that Cognitive Behavior Therapy and medication were more effective than the medication alone (NeuroHealth Associates, 2020).

Did you know that amphetamine has been used pharmaceutically in the U.S. since 1927? (Heal et al., 2013). In World War II, these stimulants were given to American soldiers and pilots to keep them alert, also known as "go pills." (Shanker et al., 2003).

Dr. Russel Barkley states, "*When you find the right medicine, you can experience substantial improvements in your ADHD symptoms.*" The medication works for at least 80% of people (Dodson, 2023). In addition, there are 78 studies on ADHD treatment by the American Academy of Child and Adolescent Psychiatry (AACAP). They all support the usage of medication instead of behavioral therapy alone (Dodson, 2023).

It's worth noting that each individual is unique, and as a result, the effects of the same medication can vary significantly among different people. Finding the proper dosage and pharmaceutical treatments can take months (Dodson, 2023).

Different Kinds of Medications

Medications are prescribed, but not to cure the disorder. Nevertheless, to create some control over their behaviors (Robinson et al., 2023). Medication for ADHD can be given to children as young as 6 years old when needed (CDC, 2022), and they are generally of two types:

♣ **Stimulants:**

70-80% of children diagnosed with this disorder show fewer symptoms when prescribed stimulants (CDC, 2022). They are the most common types of medication for ADHD, and they act extremely fast in young children and teenagers (CDC, 2022).

Stimulants are usually considered harmless for children as young as six, according to the U.S. Food and Drug Administration (FDA). This is because they help their brains control their impulses, leading to more controlled behavior and paying more attention, producing a paradoxical calming effect, reducing hyperactivity, and improving concentration (The Healthline Editorial Team, 2023). Stimulants are only prescribed by a professional. Therefore, they shouldn't be taken by kids with certain medical conditions, and your child's doctor must have their entire medical history.

The most popular stimulants include:
-Amphetamine (Adzenys)
-Dexmethylphenidate (Focalin, Focalin XR)
-Amphetamine/dextroamphetamine (Adderall and Adderall XR)
-Dextroamphetamine (Dexedrine)
-Serdexmethylphenidate (Azstarys)
-Dexmethylphenidate (Azstarys)
-Methylphenidate (Concerta, Daytrana, Metadate, Methylin, Ritalin)
-Lisdexamfetamine (Vyvanse)
✣ Non-stimulants

Non-stimulants work entirely differently than stimulants; they are neither very popular nor well-tested (Pedersen, 2021). In addition, these kinds of medications don't work as fast as stimulants, but their effects last longer, up to 24 hours (CDC, 2022).

Common non-stimulants include:
-Atomoxetine (Strattera)
-Viloxazine (Qelbree)
-Guanfacine ER (Intuniv)
-Clonidine ER (Kapvay)

How Medication Can Help in Treatment

Typically, you would want to be absolutely sure before giving your child any medication, but it has been proven that ADHD medications, principally stimulants, do work (Barkley, 2023). Therefore, when a doctor or a mental disorder expert considers your child's medical history and prescribes medication, it will be effective and help them with the more severe symptoms.

Let me tell you how medications can help in treating ADHD. Before you jump into the medication treatment plan, you must remember that behavioral interventions, physical exercise, and proper nutrition also affect your child's symptoms. Therefore, your child has a higher percentage of easing some symptoms.

Dopamine and norepinephrine are neurotransmitters inside

our brains that play a massive role in everything we face with this condition (Manson et al., 2022). Unless they function better, we can't train our brains to learn the necessary skills to go on in life, like attention and impulse control (Seay et al., 2023). We can try and try, but unless the dopamine and norepinephrine levels in the brain are stabilized, our brains won't cooperate with what we want them to do (The Healthline Editorial Team, 2023).

Whatever medication doctors prescribe will, first of all, increase the levels of dopamine in our brains (Seay et al., 2023). This will help our brains to function better and our neurons to communicate better so that we can focus on improving necessary skills (Hasan, 2018). You can help your child deal with their problems in every possible way, but you can't enable their brains to function better. Proper nutrition and medication can do that; stimulants can work on their brains in a way that no loving parent can, no matter how much you try. The correct dosage and medication will push their brain to control their impulses and increase their concentration.

Common Side Effects of Medications

The cons of medication are the possible side effects that any child can experience. At times parents think that just having their child experience some of these side effects are enough to have them out of their medication, which was what happened in my case.

According to AAP, in children, some of the most common side effects of the medication include:
 -Decrease in appetite
 -Delayed growth spurt
 -Changes in sleep patterns or sleep problems
 -Headaches
 -Stomachaches
 -Irritability when the effect of the drug wears off
 -Moodiness
 -Tics

Although none of these side effects are fatal to children, they can be harmful.

> "Children may be about one to three pounds lighter, and one-quarter to one-half inch shorter, than they would have been if not taken the medication. However, long-term studies show that even if kids do drop height and weight initially, they tend to rebound to their normal growth patterns about three years out."
>
> — DR. TIMOTHY WILENS, ASSOCIATE PROFESSOR OF PSYCHIATRY AT HARVARD MEDICAL SCHOOL, BOSTON.

There is much stigma on medication caused by the media, but medication doesn't lead to substance abuse; in fact, it's quite the opposite.

A study by Harvard Medical School examined a group of adolescents for 4 years. One group was boys with ADHD taking medication; the second was boys with ADHD not taking the medication, and the third was boys without ADHD. As a result, the boys on medication had a lower rate of substance abuse, such as alcohol, cocaine, and other illicit substances, than the group not taking the medication (Wilens, 2023).

30 minutes of exercise before school can help young ADHD individuals to self-regulate and decrease the need for stimulants, according to a 2015 study published in the Journal of Abnormal Psychology (Hoza et al., 2015). If your child is facing side effects, you must inform your pediatrician. They might change the medications or reduce the dosage.

In November 2022, *JAMA Network Open* claimed that "*ADHD medication is not associated with cardiovascular risk at any age*" (Rodgers, 2022). William Dodson called the JAMA meta-analysis "*the most important article in the last decade.*" On that note, Roy C. Ziegelstein, a cardiovascular disease expert, expressed his concerns about the meta-analysis (Rodgers, 2022): "*health care professionals must carefully weigh these factors when prescribing*

ADHD medications, especially to older adults, individuals with established CVD, and those with other comorbidities that increase CVD risk." (CVD means cardiovascular disease).

Medication might indeed be necessary in some cases, but it's also true that they should be administered with much thought and consideration.

Common Questions Regarding ADHD Medications

By now, you must have many queries regarding these medications, and I will try to answer some of them.

Are ADHD Medications Optional or a Necessary Treatment Plan?

You'll discuss with the physician whether they think medications are important for a child's improvement with the symptoms, but the ultimate decision lies with the parents.

Can ADHD Medications be addictive?

If taken without the doctor's consent, outside the prescribed dosage (higher doses for a long time), and if taken without need, medication can become addictive (Caron Treatment Center, 2022). After considering your child's medical history, only a professional can prescribe the correct drug and dosage.

Are ADHD medications a new form of treatment?

Stimulants and non-stimulants have been prescribed for over 50 years. Ritalin was created in 1944 and reached the market in 1954 (Gunnerson, 2022).

Should good parents really give medications?

If you agree to give medicine to your kid, it does not make you a bad or lazy parent. This is nothing to feel ashamed of. On the contrary, providing them with these drugs could mean that they genuinely require them.

My mother opted for medications because she couldn't find the energy to deal with all our symptoms. She was a working woman with two jobs, as well as a lot of other responsibilities on her shoulders. Although she had our father's support, balancing two young children, her employment, her home, and her relationship was still complicated.

Opting for medications doesn't mean you don't care about your child's health. It simply means that this condition can be tough to handle, and it's nice to have help when available. Because it was what our parents wanted, we agreed. I knew we would miss the ease the medications brought to our lives, but we decided to honor our parents' sacrifice.

There have been and will always be misconceptions about these pharmaceutical remedies. However, if your child's physician believes they are necessary, you should not hesitate to administer them. Your child's doctor might choose one for the symptoms but can change it to something else if they don't work accordingly. Most of the time, doctors start with one prescription, observe the child's behavior for a few days and then change the medicine or the dosage if required. It is a trial and error process until finding the optimal level, meaning getting all the medication benefits with no side effects (E. White, 2021).

Some drugs must be taken daily, while others only on school days. Sometimes, physicians might also suggest a break from them, especially if they want to assess the effect of the medicine (E. White, 2021). If there is a single side effect to the drug, no matter how small, it should be reported to the doctor. Any kind of medication should be taken seriously. **You must not self-medicate, not tamper with the dosage, and not stop taking it without consulting a doctor.**

What happens to your brain on Adderall?

I always wondered about the science behind these pills when I was younger. As an adult, I have taken the time to research them extensively to break them down for you.

Adderall is a brand name of the most famous stimulant prescription in the U.S. and is considered a Schedule 2 controlled substance (Juergens, 2023). It's a mixture of amphetamine and dextroamphetamine, which are central nervous system stimulants affecting chemicals in the brain, developed to treat ADHD (Durbin, 2022). Non-ADHD college students often use it as a study enhancer (Huberman, 2021). Athletes and people wanting to increase their focus, endurance, and productivity also misuse the drug (Kerna et al., 2020).

The ADHD brain gets distracted easily because it lacks dopamine, which keeps us focused (Boland M. Ph.D., 2021). As a result, our brain keeps searching for stimulant activities, which is where the medications come in.

Adderall takes around one hour to affect the brain after ingestion (CHADD, 2023), affecting neuroreceptors in the central nervous system and increasing the effect of dopamine and norepinephrine (Papisova, 2016). In addition, it creates a feeling of motivation, making it easier for individuals to take action to achieve their goals (Papisova, 2016).

A neurologist at Providence Saint John's Health Center in Santa Monica, Dr. Clifford Segil, states in a 2016 article, "*It increases blood flow, which makes you really excited but also puts stress on your heart.*" Dr. Clifford adds, "*it triggers the neurotransmitters in the prefrontal cortex, an area responsible for executive functioning, thus improving your concentration and focus. Then it triggers dopamine in the basal ganglia, which facilitates calm and can alleviate hyperactivity and impulsivity. And if dopamine hits the hypothalamus, the area of the brain responsible for hormone production, it can even alleviate depression.*"

Suppose an individual without ADHD takes these stimulants. Instead of getting calmer and able to self-regulate and control impulsivity, they will get hyperactive (Huberman, 2021). Dopamine levels will be increased more than necessary, creating a euphoric effect and increased levels of energy, which is why it can be so addictive when the drug is abused (The National Institute on Drug Abuse, 2021). The duration of the effects depends on the medication type and dosage and can range from 4 to 12 hours (McCarthy, 2023).

It takes around 55 hours for 10 mg of Aderral to be out of your system (Drugs.com, 2022). The other downside of the medication is that when prescribed, the drug is not concentrating on specific parts of the brain needed to improve ADHD symptoms; it affects the whole brain (Segil, 2016). Some studies have found that Adderall can increase repetitive learning tasks, but it does not make a difference in most cognitive tests or complex learning techniques, such as exams (Weyandt et al., 2018).

"Children have a brain that is very plastic, meaning it can remodel itself and change in response to experience very, very quickly compared to adults." - Andrew Huberman, Ph.D., A neuroscientist and professor at Standford School of Medicine said in his podcast, the *Huberman Lab #37* (September 2021).

So by **taking medication, children have an artificial perspective of focus created by these chemicals.** They may develop this power of attention as time passes (Huberman, 2021). The neuroplasticity of an individual between the age of 3 to 12 or 13 is the best period for the brain to be reshaped, so the earliest the child gets treated the best would be for them to achieve this level of focus without the medication later on (Huberman, 2021).

I hope you can understand more about the science behind these sorts of medications. When I was younger, I couldn't understand: if someone is hyperactive, why would they need stimulants right? Don't they need to get calmer? It made much more sense once I understood what these chemicals were doing.

What About Alternative Medication?
Treatment of ADHD consists of both medication and several exercises, but some parents have also tried alternative medication. These ingredients don't treat ADHD but can help with more severe symptoms. In this case, herbal teas, Ayurvedic medications, and a few special supplements can be considered alternative medications. Though, I advise talking with your doctor or nutritionist to see what is best for you and your child's case.

Herbal Teas: A few herbal teas, such as chamomile, lemongrass, and spearmint, are generally considered safe for children and help those who want to relax and regulate their sleep patterns.

Brahmi Capsules: Research has proven that Ayurvedic medicine works for ADHD in children and adults (Gupta et al., 2015). Brahmi Capsules, made from the extract of Brahmi plants, is a medication that works great for a healthy heart, a healthier blood pressure level, and better nerves. At the same time, these capsules are great for relieving anxiety in children (Raman, 2019).

Green Oats (*Avena Sativa*): Unripe oats are called "green oats" or "Wild oats" The extract from unripe oats can also calm our nerves and reduce stress. In addition, according to an early 2020 study, green oat extract can also boost cognitive function (Kennedy et al., 2020).

Ginseng: Chinese civilization has used ginseng extract in many herbal medicines to stimulate young brains and their functions. In a study conducted in 2011, a few children between the ages of 6 to 14 showed a drastic reduction in their anxiety and an improvement in their personality and social adjustment (Lee et al.,2011).

Pine Bark Extract: Pine barks are rich in a natural compound called proanthocyanidins, which have been documented to demonstrate numerous enhancements in children with ADHD. Among its other uses, pine bark extract reduces hyperactivity and improves concentration (Greenblatt, 2011).

Gotu Kola: Highly rich in Vitamin B1, Vitamin B2, and Vitamin B6, Gotu Kola or Centella Asiatica is nutritious for a healthy brain. According to Kesley Conger (2020), a clinical herbalist, this supplement is also quite helpful for several symptoms of ADHD, including reducing anxiety and enhancing mental clarity. It can also improve cognitive function, reduce stress and improve sleep.

Lion's Mane: Lion's mane is a natural and safe supplement with a long history of supporting cognitive health and facilitating nerve growth. Historical records indicate its efficacy and scientific studies have corroborated its benefits, particularly for children facing challenges related to learning disabilities or memory issues.

Moreover, the lion's mane possesses anti-inflammatory and immunomodulatory properties, making it a viable choice for children with chronic inflammation or allergies.

Personal Opinion About ADHD Medications

Since I have suffered from ADHD symptoms for the last 30+ years and have been on medication, I believe I am an excellent candidate to give out some personal opinions.

I did take medication for about 6 months. There were some improvements regarding paying attention at school, controlling myself more, and not getting up to talk to friends when feeling bored, which helped me focus on my studies. We felt better in many different ways than before without the medication. It was the same for my brother, as well. However, my parents did notice us being less active, which we took to be expected, but still, it was like we were different kids. Our father was the one who felt that the medication was changing our personalities, and he was not entirely okay with that. Rather, he always reminded us to be proud of who we were. I remember feeling different; even though the teachers were happier at school, I didn't feel like myself. I recall making fewer jokes and just being less of an entertaining child.

I remember my family sitting down and discussing the medication, and we decided to discontinue them. Our father concluded that the drug was changing who we were in a way. Even though it made us focus better, control ourselves, and behave more in class, it also felt like there was less of a spark in our lives. The medicine didn't make us smarter because we could still get good and passable grades (depending on the subject) before the medication. It's just that it was less of a hustle to get the homework done and cooperate with house chores. In addition, the same drugs affected my brother more, and he appeared to be experiencing sadness more frequently.

Then we decided to go off the meds, and my parents discussed it with our psychiatrist. They also asked for our opinion on it - my brother's and mine, as we did feel it was easier for us to fit in at school because of the medication. Instead, our parents requested that we try and cooperate more with their other disciplinary methods so we did not have to take these stimulants anymore; the doctor downgraded the dosage gradually so we did not have to stop completely.

So this is what I think: medications should be only administered when absolutely necessary and when the child's ADHD is not showing any improvements without them. When nothing else - no amount of exercise, brain training, or therapy - is working for the child, only then should physicians and parents think about medication.

I don't advocate giving children any medication that has not been administered to save their lives. Furthermore, any sort of medication leaves some side effects on a child's body, which should be avoided as much as possible. However, I also know the reality. ADHD children have more difficulty learning things than neurotypical children can learn easily at the same age. Some medications can certainly help with that, and sometimes, it becomes necessary to prescribe a child some. My requests to the parents and guardians reading this book: Follow your instincts; you know what is best for your child. Go after the information and make the decision you know is best.

> *"ADHD is not a choice or bad parenting. Kids with ADHD work twice as hard as their peers everyday but receive more negative feedback from the world."*
>
> — *DRB*

7

IT MIGHT NOT EVEN BE ADHD
ALL ABOUT MISDIAGNOSIS

Many people I know love reading self-help books like this. I find them helpful and enlightening as well. However, this particular book is meant to be a guideline for parents and guardians who have to deal with an ADHD kid regularly. In addition, it's intended to collect relevant research and my personal experience.

Because you see, there are two things this book can't do for your child: *diagnose their symptoms and prescribe medications.* So if you are reading this book because you think your child might have ADHD, I strongly urge that you consult a doctor for this step. Nevertheless, what you think might be ADHD might be your child, just being a child, or some other condition with the same symptoms.

Why is ADHD Often Misdiagnosed?

ADHD manifests with many different and sometimes conflicting symptoms in a child, and your doctor might misdiagnose this disorder; that is why you shouldn't rely on one doctor visit or opinion unless you trust the expert. Sometimes, what might seem like symptoms of ADHD in a child might be reasons, such as their age, gender, personality, or character traits. Confused? Let me explain this a bit.

Age/Maturity:

The youngest students in a class are usually the ones most commonly misdiagnosed with ADHD and are most likely to be prescribed medication. One 2018 study from Harvard Medical School shows: Children who start school a year early are more likely to be diagnosed with ADHD (Layton et al., 2018). If you compare the behavioral patterns of a 5-year-old and a 6-year-old in the same class, you must consider their maturity level and age.

Also, it is essential to remember that children with difficulty focusing on a particular topic are overactive and can't control their emotions. These are typical behaviors of children of a certain age.

Gender:

ADHD manifests differently between the two genders. Research often showed increased prevalence in boys than in girls. Though is now thought that prior research was poorly executed and often overlooked girls' ADHD symptoms (Slobodin et al., 2019). Parents and teachers reported in this same 2019 study that boys have more impulsivity and hyperactivity problems, whereas girls have more inattention problems (Slobodin O. et al., 2019). This is why boys are likelier to be diagnosed while girls' symptoms go unnoticed.

Problems at School:

If a child has problems at school, it could be for many reasons. For example, they could be having trouble with the lessons or the way the teacher explains things; they could be having problems making friends at school or being bullied by them. It's typical for a child with difficulties adjusting at school or in a new environment, but inattentiveness and unresponsiveness can sometimes be misdiagnosed as this condition.

Social Awkwardness:

Not all children will become popular, and not all will be friendly. Some children might be loners initially. These children have much trouble making friends with neurotypical children.

Still, we shouldn't automatically assume this is the case without considering the child's personality.

Inattention:
This is one of the classic signs of this disorder, but a child being inattentive in class can also be because of other reasons. They are daydreamers who prefer to stare outside the window all day, uninterested in what is being taught inside. It's the same with kids who doodle while the teacher tries to explain something. They might be uninterested in school or something else, such as art, video games, music, or sports.

Immaturity:
We don't expect a 10-year-old to suddenly become mature overnight or more restrained and attentive in class. When they still go on acting like a 7-year-old, we consider the chances of ADHD. Some are less mature than others. When the other kids around them have slowed down and started to act more seriously, they will experience developmental delays and immaturity. That is how these children grow up, slightly slower than others.

Sleeping Problems:
Some kids have trouble sleeping peacefully, which continues well into adulthood. Inadequate sleep leads to low energy during the day, inattention, and lack of focus. All these symptoms can be misdiagnosed when the truth is that the child is suffering from some sleep challenges.

Confusion with Other Conditions:
The most common reason for misdiagnosing this condition is to confuse the symptoms with other conditions, which I will discuss in detail next since this happens more often than it should.

What Conditions Can ADHD be Misdiagnosed As?

Sometimes, some of the symptoms in children overlap with those of other conditions. The most common and well-recognized symptoms - i.e. restlessness, difficulty concentrating and responding, and inability to stay still.

✦ Bipolar Disorder:

Mood swings are common in children, teenagers, and adults. However, when they become severe, frequent, and intense, it can be a condition known as **bipolar disorder**. Bipolar condition is characterized by mood swings that are sudden and dramatic. A child might be euphoric in a moment and depressed the next, sometimes without a specific reason.

They are also known to be deeply passionate about almost everything and have emotional responses to even the slightest change. While in neurotypical children, mood changes require a reason or a "trigger," those with bipolar disorder can drastically change their mood for absolutely nothing.

Bipolar disorder is sometimes confused with ADHD because of both cases' dramatic shifts in mood and energy levels. In both these disorders, children can reach extreme highs and lows of emotion (euphoric mania and depression) in just a few seconds.

✦ Depression

These days, the rate of clinical depression in adults is alarming, but this can also occur in children. Feeling sad and hopeless, irritated, frustrated, restlessness, losing interest in almost everything, having trouble concentrating or sleeping, and feeling tired all the time are some of the classic signs of a depressed person.

Due to the common occurrence of depression in adults and children, certain symptoms of depression can be easily misinterpreted as ADHD. So it is a logical sequence of having trouble adjusting in school or being unable to concentrate that children would start to feel depressed and unmotivated.

✦ Oppositional Defiant Disorder

Children suffering from Oppositional Defiant Disorder (ODD) defy everything to cover up their anxiety and inattention. For example, they struggle with concentrating in school, and when they can't do so, they try to cover up their inability with terms like *"I don't want to"* and *"You can't make me."* These are also classic signs of ADHD children denying their limitations by acting defiant to the world.

✦ Anxiety

It's not just adults who suffer from anxiety, but children as young as 5 or 6 years old who feel the same. Anxiety is rarely a solo disorder; it comes hand in hand with other conditions. More than 50% of children who have ADHD also have symptoms of anxiety or depression (Speyer et al., 2021).

Sometimes, anxiety is genetic and can be passed down to children from parents. In such cases, a child can suddenly show signs of being anxious all the time, unable to concentrate or sit still.

✦ **Obsessive Compulsive Disorder (OCD)**

A child easily distracted by almost everything they see around them instead of what they should concentrate on can be easily diagnosed with ADHD. However, it is also a sign of OCD, where children get distracted and obsessed with something bothering them (Saline et al., 2022). This stops them from concentrating on the task for only a few seconds or minutes until someone reminds them of it.

✦ **Autism**

Autism spectrum disorder (ASD) is a widespread condition in kids these days, and there is no way to pinpoint the exact conditions in a child. Some of the hallmark symptoms of ASD include the inability to read social cues. Many individuals struggle with social interactions. Unfortunately, as studies show, 30 to 35% of children who show autistic symptoms also go on to be diagnosed with ADHD, so these two disorders can be easily misdiagnosed (Leitner, 2014).

✦ **High Blood pressure**

Poor working memory is a significant factor in these symptoms, and high blood pressure is associated with executive function deficits, such as our memory (Saline et al., 2022). So you see, other conditions might also be mistakenly diagnosed since the symptoms are similar and quite confusing in young kids. At the same time, it might be another problem they are going through - physical, emotional, mental, or social. So diagnosing this disorder based on how a child acts or reacts without taking in other important factors can be dangerous.

. . .

How will a Professional Diagnose ADHD?

I have described this in the first chapter. Still, I will remind you of a few key points because this is very important for the readers to remember:

- Only trained healthcare professionals, i.e., pediatricians/nurse practitioners, psychiatrists, psychologists, Neurologists, Master-Level Counselors, or Social Workers, can clinically diagnose ADHD (E. White, 2021) with the help of the *Diagnostic and Statistical Manual of Mental Disorders (DSM-5)* published by the American Academy of Pediatrics (AAP) or the American Psychiatric Association (APA).
- The National Health Service in England (NHS, 2021) states that diagnosing ADHD requires a complete physical exam to rule out other possible causes for symptoms.
- Trained professionals will also interview the individual's parents, teachers, caregivers, and other adults who are essential to their lives (NHS, 2021).
- Everyone interviewed by the professional might need to fill out a standardized form known as the *"behavior rating scale,"* which will rate the different aspects of the child's behavioral pattern (Belliveau, 2018).
- The healthcare professional will also take their complete medical history and note whether the child has gone through recent significant life changes like divorce, death, or relocation in the family.
- The doctor would also note if the symptoms have been continuously occurring for at least 6 months.
- All the symptoms shall have to be present in at least two significant locations they spend their time in, i.e., school and home.

When the healthcare professional is satisfied with their

Chapter 7

research and has complete information, they can diagnose whether a child has ADHD.

"Why fit in when you were born to stand out?"

— DR. SEUSS

8

CREATE THE PERFECT ENVIRONMENT AT HOME

If you are having difficulty dealing with your child's symptoms, take a moment to think about what they are going through. There is a lot that your child has to struggle with and manage because of their symptoms and limitations. For example, they must often adjust to other people's rules and regulations completely different from theirs. In addition, schools and public places are challenging for them to change to because of having to interact with other people. Your home should be where they have to struggle the least to adjust to.

Be Consistent: Why is Consistency at Home so Important?

To a child with ADHD, an unpredictable world can be scary. These children need to be assured of everything in their life. Making their days and routines as predictable as possible is one of the best things parents do. It will give them the kind of security they need to make sense of a world that is sometimes beyond their expectations.

Consistent love, consistent discipline, routines, rules, specific bedtimes, familiar snacks, and pre-planned meals are all ways to let ADHD children know that their life at home is as secure and steady as they need it to be. These kids require assistance in comprehending what constitutes appropriate behavior for them. Since they need help adjusting to different social cues, they can't modify their behavior to fit what other people expect of them. Being consistent in disciplining children, being steady about how you want them to behave, and keeping the rules simple can make their lives compatible. Let me give you a small example.

All through the years, my brother and I had a strict daily routine that we had to follow. It went like this: *wake up-breakfast-school-home-lunch-extra activities (whether it was soccer, dance, capoeira, swimming, piano, or English lessons depending on the day)-study-play time-dinner-and-back to bed.* The routines changed only for two reasons, on the weekends and when our summer and winter holidays came up.

Since we had so much energy, my mom wanted us to be involved in as many activities as possible. It kept us active and helped us to fall asleep easily because we were so tired at the end of the day. We could manage the weekends because we were primarily tired from five days of school and physical activities, but surely we would still play with some friends. However, the vacations were an entirely different matter. We used to get more than a month of holiday each time with very little to do on those days. There were no studies or school, but an abundance of free time for us. Therefore, our extracurriculars were not very time-consuming, and we had much time left.

You would think any child would love the holidays, but in our case, we were mostly flabbergasted. It took my mother a few years to understand that it was because we had no routine to follow on those days. Like all my parents, she gave us freedom during the holidays, which only confused my brother and me more. We needed to figure out what we were supposed to do!

Unlike other neurotypical children around us, we needed a routine to follow. Even when the routine was something like play-time-nap-TV-playtime-break-playtime, we discovered something

CREATE THE PERFECT ENVIRONMENT AT HOME

as a family: *ADHD children like us always need to know what we must do beforehand.*

As you can see, a consistent routine is a wonderful gift you can give your children. Even when they are begging for more TV time or don't want to study when it's time to, having a routine to follow calms them. I have already mentioned the importance of consistency in this book, but I am doing it again because all parents need to remember. Provide your kid with a structured atmosphere at home where they understand your expectations regarding their behavior and the consequences of breaking rules. By doing so, they will develop a better sense of control over their own lives."

Why Should You Try Meditation with Your Child?

You might think: *How would my 6-year-old be able to meditate?* Meditation is not just for stressed adults juggling their careers and family or an overworked parent, but for everyone who needs to focus on their emotional well-being. The idea that ADHD children can sit and stay still for 15 to 30 minutes may seem laughable. With hyperactive children, keeping them still for 30 seconds is already challenging. But multiple studies have shown that fundamental meditation can benefit them.

Our mind is so powerful. Of course, children won't understand that just yet, but with meditation, you train muscles in your brain to think as little as possible and focus on breathing. Just like when we need to train to improve our strengths and skills in whatever sport or activity we need to accomplish, we need to prepare the muscles in our brain to improve our control over our mind.

Who would think that thinking as little as possible is so hard, right? If you have tried it before, you'll know what I am talking about: when you are there trying to think of nothing is usually when you start thinking about everything!

Some adults focus on meditation later in life, looking for relaxation or ways to adapt after quitting tobacco. Nevertheless, meditation is supposed to be a part of our lifestyle, something we lean on, if not every day, now and then, and not just when seeking help. Meditation can be a great way to teach them to calm their mind and process their feelings. In addition, it helps improve their memory and control their emotions. As little as 5 minutes a day is a good start!

Kids as young as 4 or 5 can start meditating for the first time. By this time, they have a fully grown awareness of their consciousness and can understand what is happening inside their minds. Arranging regular meditation sessions with your children at home - a place where they feel the most relaxed and comfortable - is another way that you can help them.

Meditating with your Child:
Children often model their behavior after their parents, so they might have to watch you a few days before starting. It's entirely normal if all your kids do is giggle and laugh the first few days or even seem utterly uninterested in the process. Sitting down with your child for a 2-minute, a 5-minute, or a 10-minute meditation session will take time, but it will be worth it.

Unfortunately, this method won't be suitable for every child. In fact, my parents never mentioned anything about meditation to us. I became interested in it during my adult years, but if you are trying to ease off their symptoms, you should definitely have them try. I will give you one example of how this can go.

You need to set up a nice comfortable space with pleasing aromas and peaceful music: it can be the sound of frequencies, binaural beats, or waves, something that will relax your child. Then you'll have to sit down, cross your legs with your backs straight, hands on the knees, and palms facing up. Now, take deep breaths! The hardest part of meditation is to clean our minds from everything. So, one way to approach it: *is by having your child count each breath in their head or whispering.* Whichever way feels more effortless for them is the one to take.

This way, it will be easier for them to keep their mind focused on one thing. Keep track of how long they can count without getting distracted. If they are rushing into anything else, tell them how important it is to spend a few minutes a day to ease their minds this way. It can be life-changing if they can control their minds like that.

Meditation does not have to be more than just sitting still for a few minutes, closing their eyes, breathing rhythmically, and emptying their minds of worries. I have seen successful meditation sessions and it does wonders, but it often won't be exactly every child's cup of tea. Young individuals find other types of meditation easier to practice at home, where they won't have to force themselves to do something difficult for their condition.

Active Meditating with Your Child:
The type of meditation which does not require you to sit still and focus is usually known as active meditation. They work the same way but are less restrictive, and there is much for you to choose from. Children who don't like to sit down quietly to meditate might respond to coloring together, making crafts, drawing or painting, building puzzles, dancing to music, taking walks in nature, or playing any musical instrument.

A 2004 study by Kuo Frances E. and Andrea Faber T. published in the American Journal of Public Health suggests that green outdoor activities can significantly impact individuals with ADHD by lowering their symptoms. Most of us can relate; the feeling of fresh air, between trees and singing birds, is just a fantastic experience.

These actions that we consider fun or play are ways for kids to meditate. For example, when coloring, crafting, or building puzzles, you are not actively trying to focus your thoughts; instead, it happens automatically when you are busy having fun. When a child concentrates on these activities, their mind slows down and becomes more focused. Concentrating on activities like these gives them time to calm themselves, refresh their brains, and regulate their emotions. As a result, they can focus on an enjoyable activity and have fun while their mind heals.

Mindfulness Meditating:
You can also try mindfulness meditation with your kid, but it's more suited for older children between 10 and 14. 10 minutes of mindfulness meditation with them daily should be enough initially.

Focusing on something simple as a beginner, like their breathing, body parts, or something in front of them, is all mindfulness meditation. You can also find some guided meditation programs; there are plenty of different ones, and many are free. Just a few minutes every day is all it takes, and it can help your child's memory, control their impulses and emotions, and even help them switch between tasks when needed.

Classical Music Unlocks So Much Focus:
Did you know that several studies have proven that classical music improves academic performance and cognitive function (Arjmand et al., 2017)? It can also improve your memory (Kanduri et al., 2015). A 2004 study by Oxford University found that people who listen to classical music had considerably lower blood pressure levels than those who did not listen to any music (Chafin et al., 2004). In addition, the same study suggested that the music shouldn't have lyrics and no dramatic changes in volume. It improves sleep quality (Harmat et al., 2008). It relieves pain by reducing pain perception, according to a 2018 study published in *Early Human Development* in Italy (Rossi et al., 2018).

The songs with the most favorable results were Mozart's "Sonata for Two Pianos" and Beethoven's "Moonlight Sonata." You need twenty minutes of classical music daily to improve your brain functioning (Kanduri et al., 2015). It can also decrease anxiety by increasing dopamine secretion and synaptic function.

It is also often used to assist sleep because it reduces nervous system activities (Harmat et al., 2008).

Classical music is so beneficial that if you are not used to listening to it, I suggest you start. It accomplishes beautiful things; if your child listens to it as they grow, they will benefit. I love classical music; it helps me concentrate a lot. When I need to work on a project for an extended period, it also feels like a meditation for the brain. I will cite a few composers you might have heard of that will make this experience more magical.

-Pyotr Ilyich Tchaikovsky (Russia 1840 - 1893)
-Johann Sebastian Bach (Germany 1685-1750)
-Frédéric Chopin (Poland 1810 -1849)
-Antonio Vivaldi (Italy 1678 - 1741)
-Wolfgang Amadeus Mozart (Austria 1756 - 1791)

Binaural Beats:

When I first heard about binaural beats, I thought they would be some sort of drum pattern. Though, it's something completely different. Binaural beats are less than 1000 Hz. Different frequencies will synchronize with your brain waves frequency, creating a similar experience as when meditating (Cafasso, 2021).

The research found that the benefits may have positive effects, such as reducing stress and anxiety, improving memory, attention, and creativity, and, believe it or not, slowing down the rate of brain aging (Cafasso, 2021). You should wear headphones and close your eyes for the most effective experience. So, it's worth trying different frequencies for you or your child during sleep, study, or meditation.

How Aromatherapy Can Help Your Child Relax at Home

Most of us, use aromatherapy so our homes and workplaces can smell nicer. A touch of lavender and a hint of lemon - these fragrances are usually enough to lift our moods and make us feel relaxed when we come home at the end of a hard day.

Did you know you can use aromatherapy in your home to soothe your anxious child? The pediatric nurse practitioner Vanessa Battista states in a 2018 article on the Children's Hospital of Philadelphia's (CHOP) official website that if your child is feeling anxious, under much stress, sensing discomfort and pain, suffering from mood swings, feeling nauseous, and unable to sleep properly, aromatherapy can definitely help to calm them down (Butje et al., 2008), for children over 4 years old, *lavender, orange, peppermint, and ginger* extract are safe and effective (Battista, 2018).

The lavender extract has a universal calming effect on children and adults, whereas natural orange extract is more suitable for lifting their moods. Peppermint is also an extract children enjoy and calms them down.

Introducing aromatherapy at home is relatively easy, even when you have not tried it before. These essential oil extracts are available in aromatic candles, or you can add a few drops in water to spray around the house. A few drops in your child's laundry can also give their clothes their favorite smell to enjoy all day.

If no one is allergic to strong smells, you can give your children a more comforting feel at home with some of the most fabulous aromas available in nature that will help calm them down and lift their mood.

Few things to keep in mind when using Essential oils

- Make sure you keep these away from children in a safe place; if ingested can be very harmful.
- DO NOT apply essential oils directly to the skin; you can get a product with the oils diluted as a lotion, for example.
- DO NOT heat the oil by applying it directly with flame; it can catch on fire.
- Clean the container daily when using a diffuser, preventing bacteria and mold from forming.
- Buy products from reliable sources, and do some research beforehand.

- If you have pets, ensure the desired essential oil at home is safe. Some can harm pets, namely, clove, pennyroyal, and citrus oils.

Nutrition: *You Are What You Eat!*

You might be unable to control everything your children eat outside when they are older, but you can ensure their nutrition at home. Nutrition, or giving your child the right food to eat, is a massive part of their treatment plan. As much as they need brain training, therapy, and meditation, your growing children will also need good food to ensure their health.

From when a woman is pregnant to when the baby is a school-going child, there is no denying the role of nutrition in brain development. According to Public Health Nutrition, a shortage of iron and iodine in a child's diet can lead to reduced motor functions and impaired cognitive development (Black, 2023). Similarly, DHA - an essential fatty acid - is critical for a child when learning new skills (Kuratko et al., 2013).

Other essential nutrients for a growing child, especially a child diagnosed with ADHD, include folic acid, choline, zinc, vitamins, minerals, and calcium (Ryu et al., 2022). Most parents know what nutritious meals for a child should look like, but unfortunately, only a few follow a healthy diet. So if you don't eat healthily, chances are your child won't either because you are feeding them. Therefore, please follow some of these tips on improving your meals so your child can improve their symptoms. **I recommend you ask your doctor or nutritionist to find out what is best for your case** because they will know more about what is needed after examining them. In addition, nutritionists will take into consideration their medical history and what type of meals they should have daily.

Here is a general example of a growing child's diet plan: Overall, having organic food and cutting down on all processed foods will have a massive impact on symptoms and health benefits in general.

❖ **A high-protein diet** consists of either cheese, meat, or eggs. If you are following a vegan or vegetarian diet: beans, nuts, lentils, whole grains, tofu, soy products, and quinoa are also great.

❖ Many **complex carbohydrates that help prevent blood sugar spikes,** such as vegetables, peas, beans, whole grains, bread, and pasta, are turned into glucose, i.e., energy.

❖ **Plenty of vegetables and fruits,** including oranges, pears, tangerines, grapefruit, kiwi, apples, and so on, are great for a child's brain development and growth. In addition, these are excellent sources of natural sugar. Somedays, I just eat fruits for breakfast. It makes me super ready and awake for the day, just like a smoothie.

My favorite fruits are mango, banana, passion fruit, papaya, blueberries, strawberries, and melon. Unfortunately, growing up in my family, fruits were less popular than bread with ham and cheese in the morning.

❖ Healthy **omega-3 fatty acids** are essential for brain development, and not getting enough of them may affect cell growth (Timothy, 2018). They are found in tuna, salmon, and other cold-blooded fish. It can also be found in Flaxseeds, chia seeds, walnuts, and soybeans for those following a vegetarian/vegan diet.

❖ **Good fats** can be found in nuts, olive oil, flaxseeds, whole-fat yogurt, and avocado.

❖ **Drink lots of water;** the body comprises 45 % of the elderly (Staffordshire County Council) to 78% of water in a baby, so the percentage depends on age and gender (Utz, 2000). The brain is mostly water, containing 73% (U.S. Geological Survey, 2019). 3.7 liters is recommended for men, and 2.7 liters of daily fluid is recommended for women, according to The Institute of Medicine of the National Academies (Yates et al., 2004). Dehydration can lead to poor mood and cognitive behavior (Benton, 2011).

If your child is a picky eater and barely eats anything you put before them, the necessary nutrition can also be obtained from supplements, which your doctor can recommend. It's also good to start feeding them nutritious foods as they are young and keep them away from added sugar and processed foods so that it becomes more natural for them as they grow.

I know it's hard sometimes to make some very delicious veggies. I recommend you search for recipes to make it easier for you to feed your child nutritious food. One tip is to have as many colors as possible on your plate to get a variety of vitamins and nutrients needed for your body, brain, and child.

I am thankful for having my wife come up with some wonderful nutritious food recipes; because of her, I became vegetarian. The combinations of foods are infinite, so try them out. I know how hard it is to come up with some if you are not used to cooking. However, there are so many simple, creative, and tasty recipes out there that you can find on the internet or social media.

Let me share a little fun fact about some friends of mine. They are a lovely couple: Diego from Brazil and Sigrit from Estonia, with a little boy called Solis. What a great, happy child he is! Both parents are vegan and feed Solis plenty of natural food, such as beans, nuts, fruits, and vegetables, instead of meat or processed food. Let me tell you how beautiful and satisfying it is to see a child as young as 4 love eating broccoli, cauliflower, or cabbage. For me, it feels almost insane; I remember not being too fond of those things as a kid.

So *make the change you want to see in the world!* Change your eating habits for your child; they will be very thankful in the future with fewer risks of sickness and a healthier body and mind. Unfortunately, my family did not take eating habits so seriously. Once I got older, I noticed the progress of my symptoms with my new way of living and eating.

By elaborating on the kinds of food your child can consume in moderation and those they should steer clear of, you can help them achieve better outcomes. According to the Learning Assessment and Neurocare Centre, 2013. Simple carbohydrates, because they turn into sugar, therefore will worsen the symptoms such as:

-Any type of candy
-Corn syrup in any juice or snacks
-Chips

Chapter 8

-Food made from white flour
-White rice
-Sports drinks
-Sodas
Remove all artificial additives such as:
-Artificial flavors
-Artificial colors
-Preservatives
-Artificial sweeteners

In addition, it is worth knowing the following ingredients that are code words for sugar (Stevens, 2022).

-corn sweetener
-sorghum or sorghum syrup
-sucrose
-corn syrup
-rice syrup
-saccharose
-corn syrup solids
-dehydrated cane juice
-dextrin
-dextrose
-maltodextrin; malt syrup; maltose
-molasses

Create a good habit of checking out the ingredients inside the products your family eats. Even though we know how important it is to recognize what we are ingesting, many don't realize how badly it affects our brain and health. Once I got old and started to be more cautious with the food I bought, I noticed just how bad some of the included ingredients in store-bought foods are. Also, watch out for frozen vegetables or frozen fruits. Although they are healthy choices, some brands will add artificial colors.

Something fundamental to know, which I only realized when I was older, is that when you read the ingredients on the back of a product, they are listed by quantity from highest to lowest. Therefore the first ingredient is what the manufacturer used the most in the product, and so on. An often rule of thumb is to look at the

CREATE THE PERFECT ENVIRONMENT AT HOME

first three ingredients and know what you are consuming most from this product. Therefore, I recommend you opt for products with a short ingredient list and no preservatives.

It helps me tremendously to have good eating habits. For example, I quit sodas and added sugar products, candy, chips, and alcohol a few years ago, and now, I follow a more vegetarian diet. This has helped me a lot with concentrating and self-regulation.

Unfortunately, some food we consider nutritious can increase ADHD symptoms with **food sensitivities,** according to a 2018 article by Wyatt Myers and medically reviewed by Justin Laube, M.D. If your kid is mildly sensitive to certain foods, consuming them might more prominently contribute to their symptoms.

-Soy
-Eggs
-Wheat and corn.
-Chocolate
-Beans
-Tomatoes
-Grapes
-Oranges
-Milk and dairy items

Some research shows that a protein named casein found in milk can increase symptoms of ADHD, according to a psychiatrist, professional Chef, and Nutritionist Specialist, Uma Naidoo, in her book. *This Is Your Brain on Food: An Indispensable Guide to the Surprising Foods that Fight Depression, Anxiety, PTSD, OCD, ADHD, and More (2020).* She adds that Gluten can worsen ADHD symptoms based on a 2005 study by Päivi A. Pynnönen.

> "The authors concluded that it was possible that behavioral problems, such as those that occur with ADHD, may in part be due to certain important precursor amino acids not being available until people stopped eating gluten. In certain individuals, gluten-free diets can help the body increase levels of the precursors to make serotonin, which is one neurotransmitter involved in ADHD."
>
> — UMA NAIDOO

Chapter 8

It is possible to find out if one has some type of food allergies by testing blood or skin, but unfortunately, the best way to find out if your child is sensitive to certain foods is by an elimination diet (Newmark. 2023). You can eliminate foods from the list I mentioned above for a month and see if there are changes in your child's behavior.

I am trying to avoid gluten as much as possible, and I feel a difference in a more "*ready to go*" state of mind instead of experiencing a brain fog a few times a day: absolutely no refined sugars, soft drinks, and fast food.

Other things to keep in mind:

- Have a routine with scheduled meals and snack times.
- Don't skip meals; if you or your child skip meals, these are the moments we give in and eat some junk food, so we get more "satisfied" with our hunger.
- Search what stores have more options for less processed foods in your location.
- Avoid coffee; according to The American Academy of Pediatrics (AAP), no caffeine should be consumed under 12 years old because it is also a stimulant and. It is best to keep your child from caffeine so they are less likely to become dependent.

Avoid soda. As I said, I stopped drinking it years ago, and I advise you and your children to do so as well; it has no benefits; try something like natural juice or kombucha, which is also sparkly. Research shows that store-bought and pasteurized Kombucha can be given to kids as young as 4. Remember to check for low-added sugar and mix it with water (Alexis, 2022). First, check with a nutritionist or a doctor to see if your child can have some since kombucha is a fermented drink with live bacteria.

Vitamins Essential for ADHD

The information below was collected with the suggestions from Dr. D. LeGrand Peterson, ND, in 2022 from his *Ultimate ADHD Guide to a Healthier You.*

CREATE THE PERFECT ENVIRONMENT AT HOME

You should seek professional help, such as a nutritionist, to find the best case for your or your child's case.

Vitamin B - increases alertness, energy, and dopamine.

Vitamin C - regulates neurotransmitters.

Iron - Studies have shown that iron deficiency increases the symptoms of an ADHD brain.

Magnesium - can help with brain fog, inattention, and muscle spasms.

Vitamin D - low Vitamin D levels can affect cognitive function and mood swings.

Zinc - regulates neurotransmitters and improves levels of dopamine.

Supplements are beneficial.

I will cite a few supplements that can be very helpful for an ADHD brain but keep in mind that the best way to know your child's case is to run tests, such as food allergy tests and neurotransmitter tests, and have a professional see what is the best decision to make. Again, every case is different, but if your child has a well-balanced diet, they shouldn't have any deficiencies.

Phosphatidylserine - increases dopamine levels, improving alertness, attention, and mood.

Phosphatidylcholine - helps improve memory and focus.

Rosemary - increases blood flow in the brain improving memory, attention, and focus.

Ginkgo Biloba - is a herb that increases blood flow in the brain.

5-HTP - works on the brain and central nervous system. It increases the level of serotonin.

These are a few options for you to better understand what can benefit you and your kids. Many times are very hectic, and having some tricks under your sleeves to keep up with the day-by-day can be very helpful. Proper nutrition is a fundamental part of treating your little one that you can, in fact, control at home. By maintaining a good diet and excluding everything your child is sensitive or allergic to, you can build healthy eating habits for life, one that will help them later and keep their symptoms under control.

. . .

Create a Study Space

Have a room or space where the child can only study and do their homework, free from distractions. You can make or buy a study-time T-shirt, a hat, or a study pencil, encouraging them to only study at that moment.

Give them a goal + Reward.

Remind them what needs to be done. ADHD brains like to compete with themselves. For example: set a timer for when they should be done with 3 or 5 exercises from homework. Just remember to set realistic goals, so give them a reasonable amount of time to finish their task so they can stay calm, but this will also need experimenting.

Once the homework is done on time, you can reward the child with their favorite video game; ensure they don't always have access to it. Otherwise, they will think they don't need to finish homework to play their favorite game.

Use a Fidget

We know ADHDers need to be constantly moving, whether it is shaking a leg or clicking a pen, so there are a few fidget tools that can be used to help us focus better.

Have a study friend

If your child has a friend willing to study with them, it is worth having them learn and focus together. Until they start goofing around, check on them to see if they are actually studying.

Create a Restful Environment to Sleep Better

The days we don't get enough sleep seem to drag on forever; it is hard to control our irritation or focus on anything when we are still groggy and drowsy. Unfortunately, it is worse for children who have ADHD.

These often struggle to get enough sleep, fall asleep peacefully, or sleep throughout the night. Inadequate sleep is one factor that negatively affects their ability to concentrate during the day and do well in school. Therefore, as parents and guardians, it is crucial to create an environment at home where they can rest better at night.

A lot of this is just basic knowledge that we all probably know, but still, here is a brief list of everything that you can do:

1. **Exercise daily.** Of course, we have already gone over the importance of exercising for your mental and physical health, but it is also a great way to ensure your child is adequately tired before bedtime. My mom kept us busy, ensuring we used all our energy during the day with soccer, dance, and capoeira lessons.
2. **Avoid Food that Triggers.** Foods filled with caffeine, i.e., coffee, soft drinks, candy, or foods that can create indigestion, should be avoided before bedtime. In fact, they should be avoided. Period. Any spicy food should be avoided in the afternoon and the evening, as well as anything packed with sugar.
3. **Stick to a Sleep Schedule.** Please don't wait for your child to decide when they are tired. Instead, create a routine that makes them go to bed at the same time every day and stick to it.
4. **Use Blackout Curtains.** These are great for your child's bedroom if you don't want them distracted by the lights outside at night or early in the morning.
5. With many different apps, or even on Youtube, you can find sounds of **white noise or binaural beats** that can improve sleep. Leave the phone at least 5 feet away from you or your child.
6. **No screen time before bed.** The last screen time should be at least half an hour before bed for everyone in the house. Keeping the phone away from the bed is also a good idea, so it is less of an attempt to take it as you are already in bed.
7. **Dedicate a room for electronics.** A dedicated space for electronics will make it easier for you and your child to

sleep better. You can use this room to charge your devices, play video games, and watch television.
8. **Make the House Dark.** It is not enough to make your child's room dark when they are trying to sleep. Instead, keep the rooms in your home semi-darkness a few hours before bedtime to mimic the nighttime outside.
9. **Reduce their anxiety.** Children might go to bed with many worries and stress that prevent their sleep. Talk to them, answer their questions, and reassure them of whatever bothers them at bedtime.
10. **Bath before Bed.** This is a universally acknowledged way to get comfortable at bedtime, something your child will definitely enjoy.
11. **Try a weighted blanket.** Children with ADHD have been known to find comfort in using a weighted blanket since they prefer to have some pressure on their bodies to relax.

There are many ways to ensure your home and your child are ready for a good night's sleep every day, and you must try all of them until you can find the right ones that fit their symptoms and preferences.

Take small but definitive steps toward the goal. No matter the circumstance, change tends to be uncomfortable in the beginning. However, it is vital to stay consistent and persistently strive for improvement, whether it involves new rules, chores, commandments, or adopting novel approaches to reach the desired goal. There will always be obstacles in our way, and we can't control that; **keep your head up.**

Teach Your Child to Be Grateful

Some good habits start from home, and gratefulness is one of them. Of course, there is a lot your child has to be angry or disgruntled about, but they also need to know what to be grateful about.

Everyone knows that a grateful life is linked to a happy life full of satisfaction. It reduces our stress and depressing thoughts and teaches us to be happy with what we have. Teaching your child to be grateful for what they have, is a great way to create a joyful and restful home environment.

Here are some simple ways to teach your child to be more grateful for their life.

1. **Have them Write Thank-you Notes.** If your kid is old enough to write, make them write "thank you" notes for every gift they have received or whenever someone has shown them kindness.
2. **Keep a "Thank you" journal.** To remember every time someone has been kind to them, have them maintain a journal. This way, they can read it when they feel down or anxious. This is something you can do together, as well.
3. **Thank them for their Good Behavior.** Even if it is as simple as doing their chores around the house, acknowledge their actions and show gratitude. They will do the same to others eventually.
4. **Be a Role Model.** Be thankful for everything you have been given; your children will do the same. Be vocal about your gratitude throughout the day so your child can pick up on your habit.
5. **Look for Positivity in your life.** Even in a life with difficulties, you can find much positivity if you look carefully. Throughout the day, say aloud what you are thankful for - your health, family, job, children, friends, and home. Slowly, your children will learn to do the same.
6. **Have them say it out loud.** It is extremely helpful, but adults often need to pay more attention, thinking it won't make a difference. Nevertheless, the truth is: *that*

it really does make a difference. I still do this, even if sometimes it can be strange. If they did something good such as getting ready to go to school, besides praising them with good words, have them repeat it. It will be joyful, and it will boost their self-confidence, as well as encourage them to seek that success again.

By saying out loud what you are grateful for at home, you give your child a new perception of life, manifesting positivity into their life. Your child will have many grievances and struggle more at school than any other neurotypical child. It can be challenging for them to express gratitude for certain aspects of life, often leaving it to you to help them comprehend and appreciate.

Make It Easy For them to Ask For Help.

Sometimes, the most complicated job in the world is to get your kid to talk to you or to get them to ask for help, and it doesn't happen overnight. Young kids always come to their parents with the most straightforward queries and the silliest ideas. Over time, they stop, mainly because they don't see their parents being interested in their thoughts or they get negative comments. Instead, they start asking other people, like friends, or trying to solve the problem themselves.

While it's commendable for children to attempt to solve their problems independently, their parents should still be their primary confidants and the first people they turn to for assistance. In a nurturing and loving home environment, children should always feel comfortable and confident enough to seek help from their parents or discuss any matter with them.

It is Important to Listen to Them:

The best way to ensure that is to *always listen to them, even when what they say might seem insignificant and unnecessary.* Young kids will always repeat things, talk about things parents already know, or ask questions they won't understand the answers to. Nevertheless, it is still essential that parents always listen to them, show the appropriate reactions and remember to ask follow-up questions. Then, when a child feels their words are being appreciated, they will always come to you with more.

Every Single Problem is Noteworthy:

The problems your children come to you with might not seem important to you, but it is crucial to them at the moment. So even when they seem trivial and pointless, you must listen to them and offer help. Yes, it is impossible to have enough energy and effort to respond to every single of their thoughts with significance. If you feel like you can't deal with your child's thoughts at that moment is better to take a deep breath and not answer them rudely, but let them know it is not a good time and ask them to write their concerns down somewhere so you can go back to those thoughts later.

Be Empathetic about Everything:

Be empathetic, whether they have come to you with a simple bruise or a severe heartbreak. They will understand instinctively whether you are showing real or fake sympathy, and it will determine whether they come to you with similar stories the next time. Whatever the problem is, it is serious to them at the moment, and they need to see genuine empathy in you. In your home, your child must be comfortable enough to come to you with anything and want to talk about everything.

Give Them Your Full Attention

It takes work. Parents are not just there to care for children; they also have to look after the rest of the family, home, careers, relationships, and social life. Among everything, it's tough to give your full attention when you are dealing with so much.

These kids always demand their parents' full attention. When they talk, the parents must listen and acknowledge everything they say. Sometimes, they would even want feedback or solutions. If they notice you are not paying them enough attention, it will hurt them emotionally. Eventually, they will stop sharing with you.

Your kid might feel many struggles outside with the rest of the world. Your home is a place you can make entirely comfortable for them. It can become exhausting for a parent. However, you, your partner, or the child's guardians are the ones who can make their life at home pleasant and secure.

> "When a child does not doubt that they are loved, they can, based on this certainty, sleep, dream, play, and learn. It is love that allows one to be a child."
>
> — DR. GERALDO PEÇANHA DE ALMEIDA

9

THE IMPORTANCE OF EXERCISE
SWEAT EVERY DAY!

Exercise can have significant benefits to an ADHD brain; for many people, it can be as effective as medication (Dodson, 2023). That's one of the best ways to spend quality time as a family and have fun together, but also something that will help your child's symptoms.

I am not asking you to raise a family obsessed with staying fit or lifting weights on the weekends, but anything physical can be fun and spark positive changes in your child's brain and all the other family members. Anything you do that makes you sweat and breathe harder will increase your child's attention and improve their mood.

To an ADHD brain, exercising is a kind of meditation. For some children, it is recommended to help them; for others, it is as important as therapy and brain training. Regular exercise will help your little ones control their impulses and keep them focused and ready to learn new skills. Most importantly, and I can vouch for this personally, the more exercise your kid gets, the fitter they become. Fitness is not just about being strong or trimming your waistline and looking good. The true importance of being fit is slowly losing the sense of helplessness. Becoming fit and active over time will boost their confidence significantly.

What exercise does in our brain is what certain medications

do: *increase the production of dopamine and norepinephrine in our brain.* Exercise also increases the level of endorphins and serotonin - hormones in charge of creating happiness in the brain. It doesn't just have to be rigorous exercise sessions to make them feel better about themselves naturally. There are different ways to ensure your kid gets some movement every day.

Physical Exercise is the Best there is!

Most kinds of sports that require physical exertion can be recommended for kids with this disorder, including wrestling, martial arts, track or cross-country marathons, swimming, basketball, surfing, skateboarding, soccer, and hockey. Some kinds of physical exercises, in particular, such as **gymnastics, martial arts, and the art form of ballet,** also help them to focus and manage their attention since these certain physical activities require a lot of discipline and control.

Sports can be a hobby or something more for these children if they are interested. However, not all children are interested in lots of physical exertion daily, which is fine too. You can do something physical as a family a few times a week, if not daily. Going for a walk or a run, cycling together, sending your child off to a play zone, passing the ball on the weekends, playing tennis, frisbee, or soccer in your yard - everything that keeps them physically active and makes them sweat is suitable for your little one.

Here are some tips to follow if your child is having trouble exercising.

1. **Follow a Routine.** Exercise at a fixed time every day. ADHD brains love routines and will respond better if there is a set time to exercise daily.
2. **Prepare Everything Ahead.** It makes starting something more accessible than running around the house looking for their tennis racquet or running shoes.
3. **Create Accountability.** Don't interrogate them, but keep accountability of whether they had exercised that day and how much. Instead of simply telling them to

exercise, keep an eye on them while doing it; if possible, join them.
4. **Take it Slow.** Refrain from assuming you'll make an athlete out of your child in the next 30 minutes. Instead, take your time, start slow, talk about what you want to do, and try everything until you find a favorite.
5. **Keep track of their Activity.** It can be simple, like an award chart in your home with stars for every day your child got some exercise, a bullet journal they can fill into. It is oddly satisfying how much keeping track helps.
6. **Reward Them.** It can be everything from an extra hour of TV to their favorite dinner, but instant rewards can motivate these children to do even what they are not interested in.

Again, it doesn't have to be much. The key is that your child - and you - spend some active time regularly, having fun exercising, playing sports, and just moving around, in general.

The Swing Method: What is it and How Can it Help?
We know swings as playground toys your children insist on riding for hours. However, did you know that swings can be a powerful sensory toy for their development? Sensory swings have become quite popular in recent decades, especially for neurodiverse kids. They don't take up much space in your house but can support them when feeling restless or overwhelmed.

These sensory swings can be of different types, shapes, and sizes, but they all help to make your child feel safe and calm. Some of these swings move in specific rotations or directions, helping your child to be aware of their body, work with their coordination and balance, pay attention to something in particular, and increase their motor planning. Therapists use these methods to expand their senses.

10 minutes in an appropriate sensory swing can have a positive

effect lasting up to 7-8 hours. In addition, they can be a great way to relax before your child faces any challenging situations, i.e., public gatherings, school, or exams. They are not just toys your kids can enjoy but a great way to help them calm down and work on their senses.

Depending on the sensory swing you use, you can achieve different results. Some are more intense with spins and bouncing, and others are more predictable and calming. I recommend you talk to a therapist, and they will advise on the best option to improve your child's needs. It is also essential to remember that these types of swings are not only for kids with disorders but for any child who needs their senses to be improved.

Another essential fact is: Do Not force a child on the swing because it may cause them trauma, and they won't benefit from it either. There are many types of swings, depending on age, sensitivity to movement and speed, symptoms, and sensory sensitivity, namely:

- *The versatile stretchy swing.*
- *The skateboard swing.*
- *The pod swing.*
- *The mesh swing.*
- *The flying saucer swing.*
- *The hammock swing.*

Balancing Exercises

Balancing exercises are also a kind of brain training, something so simple that your children will probably think they are playing a game! What do you do for these balancing exercises? You balance yourself, of course. I will list a few ways you can try balance exercises with your child, and then I will explain how they help.

-Stand on one foot with the eyes open. This is easy. You can even play rock, paper, scissors together like this.

-Stand on the same foot with your eyes closed. This is relatively harder and will require all of your concentration.

-Balance on a wobble board for a few minutes, with and without your eyes closed.
-Stand on one foot and put on socks on the other foot.
-Stand on one foot and pick up a few cards off the floor.
-Attempt to juggle while standing on one foot.
-Practice low plank for a few minutes with elbows on the ground.
-Stay seated on an exercise ball with your legs above the ground.

Alternatively, you can invent your own ways to balance your body using different toys and objects around the house. 30 minutes a day, and you should see some progress with your balance and reduced symptoms of inattention.

One thing I also love doing as well is **slacklining**! It's like meditation for your brain because you need to be super focused and control your body not to fall. For those who don't know, slacklining is when you walk on a tightrope between two trees, for example. The looser the rope, the harder it's to balance, and it's proven to be super beneficial for our mental health (L. Williams, 2020).

Nevertheless, like other balancing exercises, it improves stability and strengthens your ankles, knees, spine, hips, and joints. I recommend you as a parent try them as well because balancing ourselves like this is so beneficial and straightforward, principally as we age for at least thirty minutes. It also helps us achieve better posture, relaxes us, makes us forget about all our problems for a few minutes, and doesn't require a heavy load.

So why is this not a game but an exercise? A 2016 study published in the Journal of Strength and Conditioning Research shows that balancing like this can help an ADHD brain with better executive functions and spatial cognition(L. Santos et al., 2016).

The fact that balancing could be an exercise for ADHD was first discovered by Jeremy Schmahmann back in 1998. These exercises can help strengthen the cerebellum part of the brain, which is the part that is in control of some of the critical problems that ADHD brains face (Golden, 2021). This has been proven to work!

A study conducted in China 2021 had 27 ADHD patients taking *methylphenidate (*a stimulant used to treat ADHD that we discussed earlier in the book). 13 patients also received balance training, while the others only took the stimulant. After 6 months and 40 training sessions, children who had the additional balancing training showed significant improvement in the core symptoms and inattention behavior compared to those without the balancing training (Feng et al., 2021).

The evidence suggests that these exercises can potentially enhance certain ADHD symptoms. By participating in these activities together, not only can you have enjoyable moments, but you may also observe an improvement in your child's symptoms. So, it's definitely worth a try.

By this point, we have noticed that any child can improve their coordination and confidence and reduce their frustration by practicing motor skills. There are numerous choices of different activities, such as playing drums, dancing to music, learning the rhythm of sounds, playing ping pong, painting, gardening, and so on. Indeed, your kid will develop preferences and inclinations, and the earlier they begin to cultivate these skills, the more advantageous it will be for their long-term growth and development.

"I haven't failed. I've just found 10.000 ways that won't work."

— THOMAS EDISON

10

MANAGING BIG FEELINGS

You'll have to deal with one thing: *overwhelming emotions—lots of them.* These individuals frequently experience deep emotions. Joy, anger, frustration, anxiety, confusion, pain - every feeling is intensified.

We focus on some of the most cognitive symptoms and disregard the emotional ones. For example, some might know that a child with this disorder will be inattentive, disorganized, and restless in class, but their overly emotional response to everything remains unchecked.

While young kids express their feelings more than adults, ADHD ones simply "feel more." Everyone expresses themselves differently under similar circumstances. Therefore, we can't compare them and decide that some are more emotional and less patient than others. Still, "emotional dysregulation" is recognized as a symptom of ADHD in the *DSM-5-TR.*

Chapter 10

Why does ADHD make it Harder for Children to Control Their Emotions?

Everyone with this condition finds it difficult to manage their emotions. This is mainly because the delay in their brain development also delays their control over their feelings.

These kids have the same emotions as neurotypical ones, the only difference being that those emotions are more intense, more frequent, and longer lasting. Their brains can't register feelings as quickly as neurotypical people, leading to delayed emotional regulation development.

When we were growing up, we had a neighboring child who used to sometimes come over with her parents. Her parents and mine were friends, so this was a regular occurrence. She was a good kid but used to play rough with our toys. I didn't like that because I was pretty sensitive about my belongings. So it angered me whenever she would play with my toys and spread them haphazardly around the room.

Looking back, it seems normal for a young child to play this way. Tough, my reaction to the incidents did not seem normal then. I used to scream at her, a child at least 3 years younger than me. I used to make faces and call her names, and once, I shoved her away. I couldn't control my anger whenever the child came into my room.

My impatience or inability to control my anger could have been due to my condition. Still, we were just kids. My behavior caused a bitter rift between my parents and their friends, and they eventually stopped being friends. I was considered a "hot-headed boy." These kids don't intentionally unleash their anger or frustration but can't hold them in, no matter how much they try to. Therefore, parents must teach their children to manage situations where their emotions can become problematic.

How to Help Your Child with Their Emotions?

I will help you with some suggestions regarding how you can manage your child's big feelings. Instead of going about it randomly, I will choose some of the most common emotions your child might have problems controlling. Then? I will give you a few ideas of how to handle them the smart way.

Here is a list of all the expected emotions your child might have trouble controlling:

1. Impatience
2. Accepting Criticism
3. Frustration and anger
4. Fear

1. Impatience:
Impatience is not an emotion but can be intense in your kid. Unfortunately, it is one of the most common traits in these children, and restlessness will set this child apart from others. Like in the example I described earlier, your child can start to get fidgety and restless when you wait at the doctor's office with them, when you stay in a queue at the grocery store, or even when you are stuck at home. Of course, these situations make a neurotypical child impatient, but in an ADHD child, you might even have to face a complete meltdown.

Kids with this disorder will start complaining loudly, getting fidgety, screaming, demanding explanations, or crying when impatient. In addition, children of a certain age have trouble with delayed gratification, which is prominent in these kids. For example, if they want ice cream, they want it immediately.

The first thing you have to take into account here is that **you have to be patient as a parent**. If you show impatience during traffic hours in the car or at a delayed doctor's appointment, your child will pick up the same attitude. So **before losing patience, practice taking a deep breath and thinking about how you would want your child to deal with the situation.**

The worst thing you can do at these moments? Is telling them to behave, stay quiet, or say, *"People are watching, what will people think?"* No, that is not how you soothe an impatient child, especially someone with ADHD. Instead, here is what you can do:

Chapter 10

1. **Get Physical.** Most of the time, this is just pent-up energy they need to spend. So instead of making them stand, tell them to run up and down the aisle a few times, hop around or walk around the line, or do anything that will get them moving.
2. **Play Games, Any Games.** Any game would work for them at those moments, as long as you engage them in something. So, for example, play "Simon says" or "Do You see..?" or ask them to recite the days of the week or whatever is appropriate for their age.
3. **Goof Around with them.** Make silly faces, tell them their favorite jokes, and edit their favorite songs with funny words - anything to distract them from the moment.
4. **Always be Prepared.** Stay prepared with their favorite snacks, a toy, or a coloring book in your bag. Even when you are sure you'll not have to wait in line, it is always better to have emergency supplies with you.
5. **Appreciate/ Encourage their Patience.** When you see them almost getting impatient, counter with a "Wow! Someone is so patient today, just like a grown-up." This will be the appreciation they need to feel proud of their behavior, and they will try to stay quiet for a few more minutes.

It's also worth acknowledging that your child can wait. So it's good practice for them to achieve more patience. So feel free to please them whenever they want.

2. Accepting Criticism

Another personality trait in most ADHD children: *is the inability to accept criticism.* Criticisms, advice, opinions, and suggestions are what every child receives daily from almost every adult they meet, not just their parents and teachers. Constructive criticism is something we all get and need to accept. Even when we disagree, the acceptable norm is to be silent and agreeable for the moment.

When a child with this disorder is offered any criticism, most of them react angrily. Their behavior becomes visibly aggressive because they associate criticism with being a form of rejection or ridicule. To be criticized, according to them, means they are failing at something that overwhelms them emotionally. No wonder they react so badly to criticism.

There are some ways you can help them with this. First of all, **teach them to think about it later.** This is a great way to delay their reaction to criticism. They won't have to react to anything if they can train their mind to "think about it later when they have the time ." Just murmuring a generic "thank you" to the person issuing the criticism should be enough for the moment, and they can leave the situation calmly behind.

Next, **teach them to talk to you about it later.** You don't want your child to think back, analyze someone else's criticisms, and lose sleep over them. When you both get the time, you should discuss it together. This way, they can approach the matter calmly and not be overwhelmed.

Finally, for them to be able to accept criticism, **you need to practice it in your own life.** Ask your child regularly for their opinions regarding something you did and when they criticize you, accept it. Show them the right way to get criticism, and they will learn from you.

3. Frustration and Anger

The ability to deal with frustration in neurotypical brains is known as frustration tolerance, which is almost missing in an ADHD child. Frustration also builds up to irrational anger, and they can start acting aggressively.

Both frustration and anger are big emotions for these children and something they can't control without help. For example, I used to shrug and say, *"I don't care,"* to make it seem like I didn't, but inside, I did care. I would think about that thing for the rest of the day or week, whether it was a criticism or an opinion. Once I began embracing the choice of either incorporating the critique into my own growth or calmly expressing my disagreement with their viewpoint, life became more bearable. So here is how you can help them:

♣ **Teach them to express in words:**

Not screaming or yelling, but teach your child to say what they are feeling inside. Depending on their age and maturity level, it can be simply from *"I'm so angry"* to *"Not being able to express myself properly makes me frustrated, and I'm getting so angry, and I can't control myself."* This simple technique of articulating their feelings will help them better manage the situation.

♣ **Give them an Outlet**

Everyone needs an outlet to express themselves so their emotions can gradually subside without creating a scene. A creative outlet is the best in these cases. For example, your child can write about their feelings, draw pictures, or play an instrument. This is how adults usually vent when they feel overwhelmed, and they can also be great outlets for children.

♣ **Teach them Relaxation Techniques**

Simple breathing exercises, mindfulness exercises, and relaxation exercises can be taught to children as young as 4 years old so they can manage their emotions themselves.

♣ **Hit Something Soft**

Sometimes, their anger can be justified, and it is essential to let them vent. In such cases, allow them to let it all out. They can try screaming into a pillow, vent, cry or punch something soft, i.e., a punching bag or a soft toy. Showing anger is not always bad; sometimes, it can be necessary.

♣ **Create a Calming Place for Them**

Somewhere around the house where they can be alone, away from distraction, and have a safe place to think - that is what your child needs when feeling emotionally overwhelmed.

♣ **Get them to do Something Physical**

If your kid is angry and needs to vent, walk with them, run, or play something that requires movements. For very young children, you can run around the house playing catch or dancing together. It will distract them, and they will slowly forget about their anger.

♣ **Lead by Example**

Don't hide it from your kids when you are angry at something. Instead, vent your anger correctly so your child can learn from you. Do what you want them to do when angry, and they will follow your lead. It's no use telling your kid not to get angry because it's a human emotion that none of us can fully control. Instead, teach them to deal with it in a manner that will benefit them and everyone around them.

♣ **Practice Positive Imagery**

If your little one is disappointed at something they have failed or are afraid of failing something new, I highly recommend a proven practice: encourage them to vividly imagine themselves achieving their goal. By visualizing the process and successful outcome in their minds, they can significantly enhance their chances of success. You can practice with them as well. If they picture themselves accomplishing it, they have a higher chance of actually getting it done.

4. Fear

What are children scared of? Zombies, vampires, werewolves, and perhaps their TV privileges are being removed. They would fear angering their parents or getting hurt in the playground. Fear can be a complicated emotion. Their anxious nature, combined with the constant dread of being rejected, humiliated, and ridiculed, becomes a fear that no one else can understand.

I remember my brother feeling extremely anxious before any social gathering involving his school friends. When our parents hosted his birthday party one year, he couldn't sleep for days before.

"What if no one comes?"
"What if everyone lost their invitation and forgot the date?"
"What if they don't come because no one likes me?"
"What if they come and laugh at everything?"
"What if they hate my party and don't want to be friends with me again?"

All week long, he was so anxious before the party. It was more than just anxiety or nervousness. I could see genuine fear in his eyes because he worried about everything.

Fear is common in most children. Sometimes, it might seem like they are afraid of everything: *of not waking up on time in the morning for a test, of disappointing their teachers with bad grades, of not saying the right things to their friends, of making simple mistakes.* Something that seems highly trivial to neurotypical children might paralyze them with fear. Here is how you can help:

Understand their reason

However irrational your child's fear may seem, there will always be a reason behind it. Ask them about it; ask them to explain what they are afraid of and why. Ask them to draw a picture if they can't use their words.

If they are scared of a particular doll or a toy, do not force them to play with it. If they are afraid of someone who means no harm, ask them privately about it. Acknowledge their fear, try to understand it, and be patient.

Explain in Detail

If the fear is, in fact, irrational, make sure you explain it to your child. Saying something as generic as *"Don't worry"* or *"You have nothing to be scared of"* wouldn't help them. What they need from you are acknowledgment and simplification.

If your child is afraid of something, talk to them about it. Tell them why they have nothing to fear and go on explaining it until they understand. Only when they seem satisfied should you let the topic rest.

Devise Age-Appropriate ways to Banish their Fears.

We can eliminate the monster in the closet for young children by spraying some "anti-monster perfume" in the room.

For older children, you can devise other techniques to assure them, i.e., writing down their fears on paper and burning them or burying them deep into the ground, imagining funny consequences to anxious incidents, etc.

Ask for their Opinion

Before you use your ideas, ask your child what can be done to make a situation less fearful. For example, take their suggestions if they are anxious about an upcoming event or test. If you give them a chance, your child can devise clever ideas to deal with their fear.

Make them Welcome to Talk about it

Whether your child's fears are rational or irrational, they should always be able to talk about them with you. If they are not equipped to deal with the fear themselves, they should be able to count on you to understand and help them.

Fear is a natural and inevitable part of our lives; unfortunately, fear can stop us from fully living. Although this irrational and crippling fear in your child can go away with age, it is still crucial that you deal with it when needed. These are only some of the emotions your kid can go through, but they are the ones that stifle them the most. What might seem a trifle to others can be a huge deal to your little one, something you should always acknowledge and pay attention to.

You can't dismiss the idea of their emotions as being something they will "eventually grow out of" or "understand by themselves someday." As much extra work as it seems, your child's big emotions - even the simplest of anxiety, fear, or frustration they show - need to be dealt with regularly and with extra care. Hence, they never feel abandoned or ignored by you. Remember: *love them! No matter what or even if, even if they say they hate you or if they disagree with your parenting.*

The Wall of Awful

The Wall of Awful is a metaphor created by Brandon Mahan, an ADHD coach and host of the *ADHD Essentials* podcast. It's a great way to understand what people with this disorder face with their emotions, and I will share it with you. Try putting yourself in the situation because surely it can be helpful with your own problems as well as your child's.

It's essential to keep in mind that we all have our own wall, but to people with ADHD, our wall is larger than the neurotypical because of the way we deal with it.

When a person fails a task, they get a brick into this wall, a negative emotion; usually, you don't get one brick at a time, but multiple because if you fail one thing, it means you are also disap-

Chapter 10

pointed; if you are disappointed you probably think you are disappointing others, anxiety starts to kick in, and then it comes to worry and rejection, which turns into a snowball effect. So you get all these negative emotions into the Wall of Awful.

There are a few ways you can treat this wall.

- **Break the Wall.** When you get so angry that you break through it, it is one way of getting past it. However, it's not a healthy way to do it because, with anger, you can hurt relationships with family members and friends.

- **Get Passed the Wall with Negative Thoughts.** When you start asking yourself why can't you do this task, telling yourself that you are lazy when you keep procrastinating and bringing yourself down. Eventually, you might be able to do the task and get past the wall, but this is also a very unhealthy way to approach it because we are hurting the relationship with ourselves. So we must be at peace and accept ourselves to solve these issues better.

- **Climb the Wall.** Climbing the wall is already a healthier way of dealing with these emotions. Nevertheless, again, these are just metaphors; the "wall" actually means your negative emotions, so you are mentally working with these emotions within by climbing it.

Someone watching you from the outside doesn't know what's happening inside your head; they can't tell if you are working on these emotions or just piling them up.

By climbing this wall, you are talking yourself into doing this task, thinking, *"ok, I can do this,"* and believing it will be possible. Still, sometimes you are just waiting for some energy to return to you because maybe you are mentally tired and need a break.

So this is what your child can face when you command them to do something, and they take longer than you expect them to do.

So, for example, if you are telling them to brush their teeth and they are not going for whatever reason, it could be because they had some train of thought and wanted to keep going at it, meaning they did not intend to disobey you.

What would happen to me as a child in this situation is: that my mom yells at me to go brush my teeth at that moment, and yelling triggers an emotion inside the child's head that gets them past the wall by "breaking the wall."

For parents, it is hard to see if their children are trying to climb this wall, meaning trying to cooperate but just can't at that moment, or they are just staring at the wall, meaning knowing they need to do something but are just not trying to.

- **Put a Door in the Wall.** You are changing your feelings inside by putting a door in the wall to get motivated. So what is one thing that can change how we feel in just a matter of seconds? Music! Yes, that is right. Music can get us in the mood. Whether going to the gym, running, or cleaning our room, music has a massive effect on us because it releases dopamine in our brains, making it easier for us to get motivated.

Another way to release dopamine would be to eat something that excites us. As I said before, we ADHDers like to compete with ourselves. So having a timer running as we accomplish something can motivate us when we share our accomplishments with others. Also, when we exercise, it will get our anxiety away and fill our brains with dopamine.

Thou putting a "door on the wall" can be considered cheating because you can get past the wall at that moment. So you'll feel better but face the same emotions later because you did not climb the wall; you just put on a door, so it was easier for that moment. We need to work with our emotions to get past them. Have your children share their thoughts and feelings so they don't keep everything inside them, piling up these challenging emotions, making this wall bigger and bigger.

Chapter 10

. . .

Balancing Your Child's Emotions with Tips

A few tips can be of great use when teaching your children to express themselves and understand how to control their emotions by recognizing what these emotions are.

❐ **FishBowl Feeling Practice**

You'll write a few different emotions into little papers and put them into a bowl, happy, sad, excited, lonely. Maybe a feeling you think your child is facing, and you want to help them overcome it. You are then going to pick one of these papers and explain to the child how we act and feel when facing this one feeling, but you can't use the word of the picked feeling so the child can guess and label these emotions. Instead, you can connect these feelings to specific experiences your child has experienced, positive or negative. The takeaway is: that they will be able to identify these feelings when they arise and manage them more easily.

❐ **Emotions are not a Problem to Solve**

When your child feels comfortable enough to share their feelings with you, you should try and listen to them with your full attention and not interrupt them because one little thing can change, and in their head, they might think, "*oh, it's ok it doesn't really matter.*"

As they share their feelings, try to connect with them and remember ways you had to go through a similar moment that made you feel the same way. For example, you can say, "I know it is tough to feel this way, and it is hard to face this problem; I go through the same things, too," so they can connect with you and understand it is ok to feel like that. As I said, recognizing these feelings can help them overcome them better.

❐ **It Takes Practice**

Be kind to yourself; you might get frustrated because you don't want your child to be going through these negative feelings. But, remember, negative things will happen now and then, and you can't control that, but how you teach them how to handle these emotions will shape their persona.

❐ **Stay calm**

Never allow your child's mood to control yours. Instead, take a step back, take deep breaths, inhale through your nose, hold the air in for 5 seconds, and exhale through your mouth. Having the habit of controlling our own emotions puts us in a powerful position as a parent.

❐ **Walk away if they talk back.**

It might not be the case every time, but when they talk back or start crying out loud, making a scene, thinking they can get what they want by doing so. You must not give in. Don't give what they want in these situations. If they are acting out, screaming, and being rude because they want something, walk away, so it shows that misbehaving won't help them gain power over you. Otherwise, they will pick up on this method and start doing it more often.

Overall the child needs to have you as a best friend other than someone who just gives strict rules. So they are fearless in sharing their thoughts and concerns daily. If that is not the case at the moment because you feel like your child does not yet trust you to share their emotions, they should have another familiar option like grandparents or friends that could help and make the child feel more comfortable communicating their feelings.

"People with ADHD often have a special feel for life, a way of seeing right into the heart of matters, while others have to reason their way methodically."

— DR. EDWARD M. HALLOWELL

11

YOUR ADHD CHILD AND DISCIPLINE... AGAIN

Okay, so this chapter will be about something children don't love to be a part of, but something crucial in our lives: discipline. Now, discipline is what no child loves to hear, but what they need. Children need routine and organization, someone to tell them what to do and what not to do, even though they will never admit it. They know it, we know it, and everyone knows it.

Disciplining your child is not easy. It is hard for most parents to be tough on their children, knowing they already face problems everywhere else. So you would want to be lenient with them at home, where you want them to be their most comfortable. So, your home is the best place for your child to understand the concept of discipline.

Disciplining your child doesn't mean you must be harsh with them or keep them on their toes at all times. Instead, it means you need to be consistent about the rules in the house, some of which are essential for their physical, mental, and emotional development.

Children are growing up in a different environment than what used to be 10, 50, or 100 years ago. Therefore, we need to act and react differently with new ways to adapt to our surroundings, and like with everything in life; we need a balance between the extremes. There are two aspects of discipline for anyone and any situation: what is allowed and what is not. These kids seek positive attention but will overreact to the adverse reaction.

Screen Time

Let's address the issue of excessive screen time, which can be detrimental to everyone. The use of various screens, including laptops, smartphones, televisions, tablets, and iPads, is particularly harmful to individuals with ADHD."

A technology survey was done on caregivers during the pandemic caused by Covid-19. 90% of families reported that ADHD symptoms worsened in their kids, increasing anxiety (McQueen, 2022). The majority also mentioned a general behavior change that became worse than usual. For example, forcing them off the screen devices triggered outbursts of frustration and anger.

With any children, getting them off gadgets or limiting their use can be challenging. Screen time should be limited to only one or two hours daily for their own well-being. Smart gadgets have become essential in our lives, providing valuable assistance in various ways. They indeed have much to offer children regarding education and entertainment, but they ultimately harm their brains, eyes, and mental development. Any form of screen time they prefer has a few benefits that can't be denied. For example:

- These kids are primarily visual learners. Anything in a more virtual and visual mode makes it easier for them to learn than by reading or hearing about it. Therefore, age-appropriate cartoons and animations are an important part of their learning.
- Screen time can be used as a reward for completing something they are not very enthusiastic about, i.e., finishing homework and completing chores.
- Some of the most effective brain training exercises are available through apps and software. An hour of using

Chapter 11

these apps every day can help your child's development.

Despite all these benefits, screen time is still detrimental. The most significant adverse impact of spending too much time in front of screens is evident in your child's sleep cycle. If they already experience sleep difficulties, excessive screen usage can be a contributing factor. Poor and insufficient sleep can adversely affect your child's mental development and attention span.

Too much screen time can also mean issues with concentration and sudden mood swings in any young individual. Kids prone to suffer from anxiety will also be affected more because watching screens can overstimulate their nervous system and decrease their creative thinking and imagination. They will be bored without the screen, but this time is where they get creative and use their imagination. Therefore, what parents need to do is to limit screen time. Here are some helpful tips on how to do this without facing too much resistance. Given that every family and every case is different, you can implement these in your own way.

1. To foster healthy screen habits in your child, lead by example and prioritize limiting your own screen time. Practice what you preach to ensure the best results. If you've set a rule of two hours of screen time for your child, make a conscious effort to adhere to the same limit for yourself. However, it's understandable that certain work responsibilities may require you to use a computer. In such cases, try to align your entertainment screen time to be similar to or slightly higher than what you allow your child. This consistency will reinforce the importance of balanced screen usage and create a positive influence on your child's habits.
2. **Make age-appropriate screen rules.** Your 2-year-old, your 6-year-old, and your 15-year-old can't have the same screen time. It's simply not practical. Children

under 2 years old shouldn't get any screen usage apart from video calls, and kids from 2 to 5 should get gadgets only one hour a day. After they are a little older, they should be given a little more time with screens but within a limit.
3. **Set a fixed schedule that fits their daily routine, and stick to it.** It can be right after they return home, before or after lunch. However, screens shouldn't be allowed at least a half hour before bedtime.
4. **When you want your child to put down their gadgets, warn them beforehand.** Don't abruptly take away the device from them but warn them like "10 more minutes and you are done" or "One more game and you are done for the day."
5. **Follow up every screen time with some physical activity.** It can be as simple as running around, playing soccer, or catching the ball, but children should spend at least half an hour doing something active after their allotted screen time.
6. **Giving them complete independence during screen time is not a good idea.** Since their time with gadgets is limited, spending it on something productive helps. Instead of watching random videos or cartoons, ADHD kids should ideally spend their screen time doing various brain training exercises or socializing.
7. To cultivate a healthy tech environment, **ensure that all gadgets are stored out of sight when not in use.** Encourage your child to have designated personal devices that should be securely locked away once they finish using them for the day. This practice not only promotes responsible device usage but also helps establish boundaries between screen time and other activities, fostering a balanced and mindful approach to technology.
8. **Minimize the length of usage every time.** Instead of giving them unlimited screen privileges for one day or 2

hours twice a week, minimize the time they use gadgets continuously. It is better to schedule screen time for 40 minutes every day simultaneously instead of a lengthy but fewer time during the week.

9. **Play video games with them.** This is most effective for younger children just building their relationship with technology. Knowing what games they play allows you to help them process the experience.
10. **Make a plan with off-screen activities.** When boredom strikes, ensure you have other options like board or card games, walks to the park, and bike rides, so they don't seek the screens or social media first thing when they get bored.
11. **Spend some time stretching out.** Find time for a family stretch break, like a little yoga session. You can find some stretches you and your family like doing, as well as making partner stretches, and if you are out of creativity, try to search for some on the internet beforehand and write them down so you remember.

There is no way to keep your growing children away from them, but you can limit and monitor their usage. It is worth knowing that non-screen activities make us feel mentally and physically better. Nowadays, kids are getting hold of these new technologies and devices at such a young age. What used to be playing soccer barefoot outside now is playing a video game on the phone. After the COVID pandemic, we were all forced to become more attached to these types of technology because we couldn't meet people in person.

We depend on the internet for everything, which can be pretty scary, imagine, for example, what would happen if the internet crashed. We would not have access to any information by searching on a tiny little screen. So we must use this technology to protect our well-being and health and understand where the limits are. That is why I want to help people comprehend the balance of screen technology. Studies have proven that sleep problems at an early age can develop psychopathology (mental disorders) in children and teens:

- Screen time significantly affects the brain and insufficient sleep duration.
- Watching tv shows or playing violent video games before bed also negatively affects sleep.
- The use of light-emitting devices before bedtime decreases sleepiness and increases alertness.
- Screen usage causes a delayed release of melatonin in the brain (the sleep hormone), making it harder to fall asleep.

Limiting screen time to only a few hours every day can be the perfect balance your child needs. Start these habits early on so you can avoid future problems. If you have yet to try some of these tips, there is still time.

Empower What Your Kid Controls

Remember, your kids are in charge of their own choices; unfortunately, you don't control everything, so **you give them a choice by empowering what they control**. It's okay to say, *"You know what, darling, that is your choice."* Empowering their choice and honoring them also means there will still be consequences that children can't control. By doing this, you can also understand your child's maturity level.

Let me give you an example. If you give your child twenty minutes to play on the slide, you must tell them that when they are done, they must go home without recitation because that is what you agreed on. Make sure to make it straightforward for your child to understand the requirements.

Tell them it will make you unhappy if they don't follow the instructions. Once the time is almost up, you'll give your child a heads up so they are preparing mentally to stop playing soon, 5 more minutes, 3 more minutes, then 30 more seconds. Once the time is up, you'll tell them, "*Okay is time to go.*" This will be challenging for any kid, principally with ADHD, who has difficulty managing time. Suppose you practice this, and your child can understand they control whether they will stop playing. In that case, chances are they will have more self-control and know they could stay, play more and disobey, making you unhappy, but they can choose to obey and stop playing after the 20 minutes.

Empowering their choice does not mean you give them what they want, but you acknowledge they will do it. One option is to yell and tell them to leave now and that they can't stay longer. In reality, they can stay, but that would lead to some consequences because, after all, they would be disobeying you. If so, you need to follow through with the consequences, which they don't control, because you are in control of punishing the child in any way.

So if your child obeys and comes with you, tell them, "*Sweetie, it is great that you are making mama happy.*" So you are empowering their choice. This way, they will appreciate that you gave them an option and honored their choice. Perhaps it is still complicated to understand, so I will give you another example scenario:

> Mom: "Alright, it's time to start getting ready for school. Remember, we need to leave in 30 minutes, so let's focus on getting dressed and having breakfast."
> Child: "I don't want to go to school today. I'm too tired."
> Mom: "I understand that you might be feeling tired, but going to school is important. Let's try to get ready as quickly as possible so we have some extra time to relax before we leave."
> Child: "But I don't know what to wear."
> Mom: "That's okay, let's pick out two outfits and you can choose which one you want to wear. How about this one and this one?"

Child: "I like the blue one."
Mom: "Great choice! Now, let's go brush our teeth and hair."
Child: "But I don't want to brush my teeth."
Mom: "I know it's not your favorite thing to do, but we need to take care of our teeth. How about you choose which toothpaste you want to use?"
Child: "I want the strawberry one."
Mom: "Okay, let's use the strawberry toothpaste and then we can have breakfast."
Child: "I don't want cereal."
Mom: "That's okay, what would you like to have for breakfast?"
Child: "I want pancakes."
Mom: "We don't have time to make pancakes this morning, but how about some toast with peanut butter and banana slices? That's quick and easy, and still delicious."
Child: "Okay, I guess that's fine."
Mom: "Great! Let's finish up breakfast and then we can get our shoes and backpacks on. We're doing a great job getting ready on time, and I'm proud of us for working together."

This example shows a mom empowering her child by giving them choices and allowing them to control their morning routine while maintaining structure and expectations for behavior. The mom also uses **positive reinforcement and encouragement to help the child stay on task and feel motivated**. It's not easy and will take practice and patience, but you can experiment in different situations to empower their choice.

Listen! Rather than Argue

Arguing with kids gives them a false sense of power, so

listening rather than discussing will ease your relationship. Whenever you feel like your child is about to start an argument against you and they seem unhappy or angry, take a step back, take a deep breath, and take a listening approach, where you say something like, "*oh, that's interesting; tell me more about it.*" That alone might throw off their game because they expected you to start arguing or yelling.

It will change the dynamic of the conversation from an argument to a dialogue, already a healthier relationship. Also, you'll show more empathy to your child, having them understand more that you care about their feelings. Work on one behavior problem at a time. There are a few other ways you can deal with when they are acting up or trying to argue with you; you can walk away. **Do not feed the fire.** It does not make you a bad parent by doing so; you are making a statement that they gain no power and have no control over the situation.

Suppose they are aggressive with others, which can be something that happens quite often with ADHD boys. Start by asking him, "What were you thinking before you hit your colleague?". So you can discuss the other options around it without violence.

Teaching about Consequences

Young children don't care about the consequences of their actions. So it is not precisely because they are insensitive or inconsiderate but because they are children and can't think very far ahead. They might seem like they don't care about what happens and ignore your warnings or threats. For example, you threaten them with no desserts after dinner or no more TV privileges for the rest of the week, and instead of listening to you, they roll their eyes and walk away. It can be frustrating when you try to discipline them, and they are not even paying attention to your warnings.

There could be four different reasons for this:

- They are trying to stop you from holding onto the consequences. They are trying to derail you from

following through with your threat. In their mind, if you think they don't care about the consequences, it does not matter whether you take your warnings seriously.
- Your child might feel helpless; they might think the outcome will be the same whether they follow the rules or not.
- They don't believe you. You have not followed up on your warnings the last few times, and now they think your words are no good. If you constantly threaten to take away their toys or video games but end up not doing it, your children won't believe it the next time.
- Alternatively, your child might be dealing with depression which can be pretty serious, where they actually don't care about the consequences. They are not just saying things like *"Whatever"* and *"I don't care,"* but that is how they really feel.

Whatever the reason, it's hard to discipline a child who doesn't care about what happens when they break the rules or doesn't fear the punishment. This really shouldn't be allowed to occur at home. Your child needs to take the regulations seriously and respect the consequences you set for them. I am going to teach you a few ways to ensure that.

- **Call their bluff** if you think they are just acting like they don't care to derail you. When they say they don't care about you removing their toy or TV privileges, stick to the punishment. Say something like, *"That's great. You won't be upset, then. I'm relieved,"* Then do what you told them you would do if they didn't behave.
- If you think they don't believe you, **follow through.** They have no reason to believe you if you are not sticking to your words. Whatever privileges you have threatened to take away, do it when they are not following the rules.

Chapter 11

- If your child thinks their actions don't matter because the consequences depend on your mood, **it's time to change your parenting style regarding discipline.**

For example, the consequences of lying in your household would be severe, like taking away their toys or missing out on a party. Instead of being consistent in your punishment, you treat this offense differently every single time. Sometimes, you let go of the matter when they have been caught lying and punish them severely. This could be why your child thinks the consequences will depend on your mood and not on anything they say or do. If this happens in your home sometimes, **you must consistently warn them.** Your children should know the exact consequences of lying, which should ideally be the same every time.

- If you think your child might really be depressed and don't care about the consequences, **you must discuss this with their counselor or physician.** The matter can be severe, and some therapy might be necessary for them, so you must deal with the issue immediately.

Your kids must know their boundaries regarding discipline and what will happen when they step out of line. Children with ADHD don't usually break the rules and misbehave intentionally, so they must be aware of the limitations and consequences.

Rewards for Good Conduct
These are simple ways you can ensure your disciplinary methods are being understood, observed, and respected by your children. Every home is different. Some families have a rigorous set of rules they follow, while others are lenient about mostly everything except a few concrete rules. In a family, young children obey their parents and other guardians' management, most of which is for their well-being. In most families, discipline is simple:

reward and praise your child when they listen to you, follow your instructions and do well in everything.

How do Rewards Help?

Rewards make tasks more interesting; instant rewards motivate children to follow instructions. These days, parents don't believe in rewarding their children with toys or gifts but with privileges. For example, promising a child a trip to their favorite play zone or favorite activity is a reward that will motivate them to do almost anything. These children prefer instant gratification instead of long-term goals.

Let me give you an example. Ice cream after they have finished their homework or a trip to Disneyland if they complete all their homework for the rest of the year – which one do you think your child would choose? In most cases, they would choose the ice cream because they can understand instant rewards more than they can teach themselves to wait for the reward for a year.

Rewards must be instantaneous, visual, and visible. Acknowledgments and encouragement are fine, but these children need something they can see, measure, tally, and preferably touch to understand its significance. There are a few ways you can reward these kids.

✦**Sticker Charts**

Psychologists recommend stickers or behavior charts for preschoolers with ADHD to modify their behavior. This is a simple way to encourage proper behavior at home and school without overwhelming them.

Note the behaviors you want your child to notice on a whiteboard or chalkboard. For preschoolers, pictures would be more suitable until they learn to read. Whenever they have followed a particular rule or achieved a goal, a tick mark or a sticker goes up to the board, marking their success. When they have fulfilled all their daily goals, they can get a reward, something simple like family game time, their favorite dessert after dinner, or a different story at bedtime.

Every *"I finished my homework by myself"* gets a sticker.

Every *"I've listened patiently to my teacher in class"* gets a sticker.

"I've finished my dinner before asking for dessert" gets a sticker. A sticker chart can be their goal for the day or the entire week. The idea for sticker charts is ultimately customization for every family, giving the child a visual motivation for what is expected from them. Whatever goals you want your child to achieve, put them on the sticker chart, and they will be motivated to complete them faster.

✦**Raffle Tickets**

Raffle tickets work the same way as sticker charts. Just like you get raffle tickets by playing games in an arcade which you can later exchange for a toy, your child can exchange their tickets for something they want.

This technique works better for slightly older children because it involves a few calculations. For example, accomplishing smaller tasks like tidying their bed or cleaning their desk may earn them one or two tickets. In contrast, more significant undertakings such as finishing homework or aiding with household chores may reward them with five tickets. At the end of the day, your child can exchange their raffle tickets for a privilege, which will be decided by the number of tickets they have collected.

Sounds complicated? Let me explain this technique a bit. First, you must assign a particular number of raffle tickets for each task you want your child to complete. Something simple that they are okay with doing will get them one ticket, a task they must be reminded of every time. Give them two tickets if they can complete it without being reminded. Suppose something they don't like to do will give them up to five tickets.

At the end of the day or the week, you can count the number of tickets they have collected.

They made their bed without being asked. Two tickets.
They brushed their teeth. One ticket.
They woke up by themselves after hearing the alarm. Two tickets.
They finished their vegetables. Five tickets.
Completed homework by themselves. Five tickets.
They completed their chores after school. Five tickets.

A total of 20 tickets at the end of the day can give them a preappointed privilege, something simple like choosing a movie for family movie night. Your child can also choose not to redeem the tickets daily but save them for something bigger. 200 raffle tickets can get a playdate with a friend, or 500 tickets can get a new toy. In other words, the children attempt to create savings to buy them something they want, just like adults save money to treat themselves to something nice.

Like sticker charts, this is also a customizable technique that completely depends on your family and your child's needs. The raffle tickets can be printed out at home or made yourself from colorful paper, but something visual and concrete that your child can see and, in this case, hold in their hands, save and spend.

◆ **Verbal Acknowledgment**

Modern rewarding systems are great and genuinely work, but nothing beats the verbal acknowledgment your child needs from you. All kids need their parents to witness everything they do. This is why you can see young children running up to you to exclaim something as mundane as *"Did you see that cat yawn?"* or *"Did you see that airplane flying in the sky?"* Almost everything fascinates them, and they want to share it with their loved ones.

It is the same with all the tasks and chores they must complete. If they have done something that is expected of them and falls under their responsibility, they would still want it to be acknowledged. It is the purest form of attention they want, for their actions to be noticed by everyone.

So whether you use a sticker chart, raffle tickets, or any other technique that motivates your child the most, it should be accompanied by verbal acknowledgment. Even something simple and small that does not have a place on the sticker board or deserves a ticket should be acknowledged with a *"Well done!"* or a *"Good job!"* Verbal acknowledgment and praises motivate any child more than anything else. Unfortunately, children with ADHD usually suffer from low self-esteem because they are unsure of how to behave or act in most situations. Simple words that don't require effort will mean the world to your little one.

✦What Should Your Rewards Look Like?

Rewards don't have to be expensive or unique; they don't even have to be something you buy. However, they must be something your child loves, wants, and is willing to work for. I will give a few examples of your child's reward.

1. A fun activity to do together as a family. Like going to eat out on the weekends, going on a road trip together, a family game night, movie night, etc.
2. Cash is not a bad thing unless you are showering them with more than they need. A few dollars for a week of chores completed or after they have helped you make a meal can be a great motivator. Just like the raffle tickets, your child can use the money to buy something they want.
3. A playdate or a sleepover with their friends.
4. Quality time with one family member where you do something special together.
5. Additional screen time can be offered as a reward, but only a little.
6. A sweet treat, making the dessert they like, even something you don't usually serve at home, like ice cream.
7. Something from their wish list, within reason.
8. Hugs and cuddles that your child is definitely going to love.
9. 30 more minutes before they have to go to bed, a chance to stay up with the grown-ups.
10. An additional story at bedtime.

The rewards you offer your child don't have to be much, but

they can still motivate them to behave the way you want them to act.

Punishing your Child

Now, let's come to the other side of the coin: *punishments.* In my culture, physical punishment was not thought to be wrong. Instead, they were encouraged to "discipline" children. Though these days, parents are much more sensitive and accommodating. Of course, hitting your children is unethical, but still typical in different cultures. It has been proven that rewards work better to motivate them to follow the rules. At the same time, the concept of punishment has changed entirely from what we know from our childhood. Some psychologists say it is better to use only rewards and not punish the ADHD child just because they respond worst to punishments. So I recommend you experiment and try different things.

For example, if your child isn't behaving, instead of focusing on what they did wrong, focus on what they should have done instead. It is pretty complicated because you still need to be strict with them. Otherwise, they will think it is okay not to follow the rules. Instead of saying/yelling, *"you are never listening to your mother!"* try asking, *"why didn't you do what I asked?"*

Still, sometimes your child will require some form of punishment, usually implemented by taking away some of their privileges. Unfortunately, regular modes of punishment don't work for children with ADHD because they can't regulate their emotions. For example, punishing a neurotypical child might force them to behave the next time. However, an ADHD child will only feel guilty and ashamed, making them angry for being unable to control themselves.

Research has shown that corporal punishment, such as spanking, can lead to mental health issues, substance abuse, and intimate partner violence down the road. Have you heard of the saying *"violence creates violence?"*. We can not teach the next generation that we can solve things with violence; we need to

Chapter 11

end it. The same thing goes for harsh verbal disciplinary methods.

You need to be your child's best friend. You are working together on being the best version of yourselves. You have so much to teach your kid. You also have so much to learn from them, a beautiful thing you understand only when you become a parent.

So having a healthy relationship without violence is an excellent approach to parenting. I am happy that, in my case, I turned out to be a very disciplined person; once we were off the medication, my brother and I started working together to make my parent's life easier so we could have it more accessible as well. My parent's co-workers always complimented us, saying we were such behaved and polite kids, which I am pretty proud of; once your little ones notice that by cooperating with you, things will get easier down the line. Life will always hit you with obstacles, which I am sure you know, but the good moments keep us going.

How to Punish Your ADHD Child?

Time-outs, taking away their privileges or toys, grounding them, restricting their social life – these disciplinary methods won't work with an ADHD individual in the long term. Disciplining them is more about rectifying their wrong behavior without exactly having to punish them. No wonder parents are usually confused about how exactly to do that. Why don't I give you a few ideas? First, **you must understand that sometimes your child is not doing this intentionally.** ADHD is a neurodevelopmental problem. So if they are disrespectful or disobedient, it is because occasionally they can't control it.

Secondly, **instead of judging their actions, find the reason behind them.** Most of the time, there would be an unmet need behind your child's misbehavior, and you must meet that need. Chronic behavior and impulsivity – are usually the main reasons behind their misbehaving. Isolate the reason behind their actions, and you can rectify them without actually punishing them.

Thirdly, **you can appropriately use time-outs.** These kids

165

don't understand the concept of time-outs, and any punishment will make them feel guilty. Time-outs can't teach your child how to behave, but you can use them to calm them down. For example, if your child is throwing a tantrum, you can tell them to spend some alone time until they can relax.

Finally, **make your expectations known, and your kid won't defy them.** Any concern dealing with the child's attitude is an ongoing process; you need to repeat and implement other ways to improve it; each incident will have a follow-up with a consequence, such as losing their favorite toy until he apologizes to their colleague.

There is something I still suffer from, though it was worse in my childhood. Whenever anyone would give me instructions or tell me something important while I concentrate on something else, I won't remember what I was told! Because we are very focused on one thing we are engaged with at that moment, it is hard to concentrate simultaneously on what we are being told. As a result, children might hear the instruction but not really listen to them.

My mom later devised a plan: when she told me I had something to do, she would first ask if I had understood. Most of the time, I would say 'yes' without hearing her question so she would stop talking to me and I could concentrate on what I was initially doing. My mother would then ask me to repeat the instructions as she mentioned, and oh boy! How many times did I not remember what she had told me? I highly recommend implementing the following technique: ask them to repeat your instructions. By doing so, they significantly increase their chances of remembering the instructions, leaving no room for excuses later on.

> *"Behavior isn't something someone has. Rather, it emerges from the interaction of a person's biology, past experiences, and immediate context."*
>
> — *L. TODD ROSE*

12

DEALING THE REST OF THE WORLD

You can see how these children suffer from social interactions and how difficult it is to make friends or be around new acquaintances. Your child can be shy, but it can also be because of their disorder. Social anxiety is a big part of ADHD. It's hard for these kids to make friends with other neurotypical children or to understand complex social norms, mainly because some of their core symptoms make it very complicated for them to function appropriately in social gatherings:

1. They have trouble sharing with friends.
2. They don't understand how to behave in certain social situations.
3. They can't follow instructions correctly, which hinders their ability to play along.
4. They can be socially awkward.
5. They might blurt out something which can sound offensive to others.
6. They can't take rejection or criticism easily.
7. They are intrusive and may ask insensitive questions, eavesdrop, or demand to know everything.
8. They have trouble waiting their turn for anything.

9. They are usually withdrawn and might not want to answer any questions sometimes.
10. They might suddenly start acting aggressively with others.

It doesn't necessarily mean your kid won't make friends or have trouble with their peers. However, they might need help in situations they can't handle themselves. A huge part of taking care of your child is to help them deal with the rest of the world, the people who want to be their friend, and the negative people they will face.

Making Friends

Not all children have problems with peer friendship, but some do. If this is an issue with your child, you must take the first steps to solve the situation.

Help them make friends.

If your kid s timid, they will have trouble making friends alone. This is fine with very young children as the parents are the ones who usually can help with this. If your child is young and just starting school, keep in touch with the other parents of their classmates. **If they can't make friends, you can do it for them.**

How? **Arrange playdates, invite other kids to your house with their parents, and do whatever is needed to make them feel comfortable.** Reflect on each playdate and ask your child whether they enjoyed it and if they want to ask that friend back again. You might make introductions, but you must value their opinion.

You can reach out to other parents for this. If your child has any particular social issues, talk to the other parents about them. Arrange play dates based on mutual acceptance of the situation. Please reach out to families with sensitive children instead of children who are loud and demanding. **Your child's teacher can help you with this too.**

Ask your child whom they want to be friends with, and

Chapter 12

contact the parents of the children they name. Take it slow and ask for their opinion and experience with everything. When arranging playdates, **it is better to do it at home instead of someplace new.** Your kid will be more comfortable and more in control of themselves in familiar surroundings. Even if you are tempted to let them go to someone else's house for a playdate, do it later when they are ready.

It takes your kid more time to make friends, and you have to be there every step of the way. Staying with them at all times can be frustrating, but it is necessary initially. Here are a few more ideas to help you:

1. **Start with one-on-one playdates.** Instead of arranging for a large group to meet, only choose one or two of their friends. Let the playdates start small with only a few kids so your child feels more comfortable.
2. **Seek out younger kids.** ADHD individuals are mentally less mature than neurotypical ones their age. They can engage better with children a few months or years younger than them. If their classmates have younger siblings or if there are younger children in the class, they can be the ideal playmates for them.
3. **Keep them short.** Your child might complain that the play dates are concise, but they can't handle anything longer than 3 or 4 hours. Any longer and they will get tired and start fidgeting, and their mood will deteriorate. It is better to keep the playdates under a few hours every time.
4. **Set good examples.** Take your child along when meeting your friends, whether they have kids or not, if appropriate, of course. This way, they can learn how you interact with your friends and follow your example.

With each social interaction, your child will grow more and

more confident and learn to make friends by themselves. Until they do, they need your help to get there.

Keeping Friends

Now, it is easier to make new friends than to keep them. With young individuals, a 5-minute conversation makes new "friends," but as adults, we know how hard it is to keep them. Children fight and then make up, but sometimes they do drift apart from each other. Unfortunately, a child with ADHD can't deal with rejection from their friends. Just as your child requires assistance in "making friends," they will equally benefit from additional support in "maintaining" those friendships.

Just as you reached out to other peers and their parents to help your child make friends, it is also your responsibility to reach out to them to foster a bond, prevent conflicts, and maintain positive relationships.

Here are some of my tips:

1. **Always keep an eye on their interactions.** Avoid intervening unless necessary, but it is important to remain vigilant about what occurs between your child and their friends. Arranging playdates at your house is one way to do this, or ask them regularly about their friends.
2. **Know the signs.** Conflicts in young friendships occur over the simple stuff really: *someone not willing to share, telling a fib, tattle-tailing, or aggressively picking up a fight.* Whether it is your child doing this or one of their friends, intervene before things get out of hand. Distract them, change the topic, give them a snag, or suggest a game - do whatever is needed to diffuse the situation.
3. **Beware of Competitive Spirit in the Group.** These kids have always had trouble with competitive play. They tend to gloat when they win and rage when they lose - both qualities not appreciated by other children. This is where you have to intervene again or encourage

Chapter 12

games that don't require playing against their friends but with them. Too much competition leads to conflict, and that can ruin friendships.
4. **Be okay with having just one or two friends.** Your child doesn't need a big group of friends or multiple groups. Having only one or two good ones should be enough when they are young, so there is no need to panic about it. This is better because your child can concentrate on each friendship more.
5. **Follow their Interests.** Encourage them to find friends - or do so yourself - with similar interests. If your child is genuinely shy, they will have more to discuss with children with a common interest. It can be books or games, music, or the right kind of toys, but they help the conversations and minimize conflicts.

Most importantly, there is no need to worry so much. Your child might need more time and even go through a few heartbreaks, but they will make friends just fine. In the meantime, they need your help and guidance.

Dealing with Bullies

Unfortunately, most children have to deal with bullying. Bullying can be everywhere at school, at home, in your neighborhood, and in your own family. It's an inevitable part of every childhood. Bullies usually target children who are different, stand out, are physically or mentally weaker, and suffer from social skills. Kids with this disorder fall under all these criteria and become bullies' ideal victims.

Furthermore, sometimes these children can become one after being bullied for years. You have two jobs: *teach your kid to stand up to bullies and stop them from becoming bullies themselves.*
Standing up to Bullies
There is no denying the fact that your little one may fall victim to bullying, not just at school but everywhere else. As much as you

try to shelter them from the negatives of life, the best thing you can teach them is to stand up to the adversities.

Every situation is unique; every bully is different. The best I can do is to give you some ideas you can impart to your child against bullying.

- **Be attentive to indicators.** Children rarely approach their parents or teachers and directly express, "I'm being bullied." Most of the time, they believe they receive the mistreatment they deserve due to their dissimilarities or that no one will take them seriously. Therefore, it is up to you to identify the warning signs.

Bullying is something that needs to be handled delicately. Ask your children about school or play dates and their friends; ask what they talk about or how they treat them. If they seem reluctant to talk about someone in particular, it could indicate a problem. You can gather the story from other children, teachers, and parents (or, if this is not in school, other people) to confirm your suspicion.

- **Define Gender Roles.** Bullying is different in the case of boys and girls. While boys tend to be more physically aggressive, i.e., shoving and pushing, girl bullies use their words. Both are two different kinds of bullying, which can be severe. Don't take it lightly if your child is not being pushed or shoved but called names by others. Discounting the incidents because *"nothing serious"* has occurred can be more traumatic for your little one.
- **Involve authorities.** Never shy away from involving teachers, other parents, or the school's principal if your child is being bullied. Older siblings or their friends' siblings can also monitor the situation. Since you can't be in the school to intervene, other authorities can do it on your behalf, so the problem is manageable.

Chapter 12

- **Be accessible when they want to talk.** Be the first person your child comes to when facing anything in life, be it bullying or other negativities. How can you do this? By always being ready to listen to them, by giving importance to any little grievances they have, and offering solutions to minor problems.
- **Figure out the Triggers.** There might be some specific reasons others are bullying your child, i.e., when they talk too much in class, are affectionate to the other children, criticize others too much, or offer unwanted opinions, etc. Although this does not excuse the bullies' actions, knowing the triggers can help.

If your child is doing something that might not seem appropriate to others, they should be made aware of it. Then, they can control this particular action, or you can discuss the situation and take it with the authority in charge.

- **Avoiding bad attention.** Standing out from the crowd is not wrong, but your child will lead a more peaceful life if they can *go with the flow*. If something in particular about them attracts a bully, like tattling to the teacher, complaining about everyone, or blurting out the answers when not asked, these are habits that should be controlled. Although bullying is never pardonable, it is not a good idea if your child is trying to attract a bully's attention.
- **Teach them the right way to react.** Let's assume the bullying will continue, so they must know how to respond ideally. Depending on your child's age and maturity level, here are some approaches they can try:
- **Use humor and make fun of themselves.**
- **Agree with the bully and thank them for their suggestion or idea.**
- **Answer back in a sarcastic tone.**
- **Avoid the bully entirely and don't react.**

- Ask back: *Why would you say something like this?*
- Ask for an explanation.

These are great ways to diffuse any situation with bullies or negative people in your child's life.

- **Involve the bully's parents.** Sometimes, your child's bully can be utterly clueless about their actions. Involving their parents directly or through a teacher can be an excellent way to ensure everyone is aware of the situation. The bully's parents can take matters into their own hands, rectify the issue, and even make them apologize to your child.
- **Help your child to recover.** Dealing with a bully can leave your child doubting themselves and their other achievements in life. This is where you can step in to remind them how special they are. Highlight their other successes, whereas the bully has only highlighted their shortcomings. They could be anything from your child's academic achievement to their creativity, manners, or hard work to improve themselves.
- **Teach them the differences.** Sometimes, your child is facing teasing rather than actual bullying. Since children with ADHD are sensitive to criticism or rejection, they might consider everything their friends do to be bullying. This can make them social pariahs if they cry off to the teacher when the other children are not bullies.

Talk to your children when upset about anything, and try to understand the situation. Is it bullying or just innocent fun that your kid misunderstands? Explain their friends' real intentions to your child and teach them to be a part of the joke.

Unwanted as it is, bullying is, unfortunately, a part of all our lives. Even as adults out of school, we will face bullies everywhere - in our family, among the people we consider our

Chapter 12

friends, and in the workplace. At some point in our lives, we must learn to confront our bullies; therefore, it's always preferable to begin early. Thankfully, with you guiding them, your child will learn to stand up to, ignore, or deal with their bullies someday.

You can't avoid your child facing bullying, and it will shape your child into adulthood. Having them talk about it and trying to solve the issue is the best thing you can do instead of ignoring it. Ignoring bullies or taking their words into your heart - both attitudes might scar them for life. Sometimes your child won't want to share everything with you, but maybe they will with their grandparents or other family members. Whomever they choose, they need to let it out one way or the other.

It depends on our emotional and intellectual maturity level and how we deal with it. Every child is different, and they will tackle the situation differently. The best you can do with your child is to help them.

When Your Child Is the Bully

Incredulous as it sounds, your child can become the bully if you are not careful. As a parent, you might be relieved when your child is not the one *being bullied,* but it may be more worrying when they *become the bully themselves.*

With all the symptoms a child with ADHD shows, it's difficult to imagine them as bullies. However, it does happen, and neither scenario is desirable.

Why does this happen?

The culprit is the same characteristic in an ADHD child that sometimes makes them the target for other bullies: *impulsiveness.* Because these children are impulsive in nature, they are usually the ones who act out aggressively against their peers.

Here is how you can recognize if your child is being the bully:

- They will show a lack of empathy for others. Even though they are sensitive, they won't show compassion

to others and often try to blame them for their mistakes and wrongdoings.
- They will be obsessed about fitting in and willing to do whatever it takes.
- They seem excessively angry and frustrated lately with no concrete reason.
- They tend to put others down, insult others, and bad mouth them, calling their classmates names.
- They struggle to control their emotions, both positive and negative ones.

If you suddenly see these changes in your child and start getting complaints from teachers and other parents, it could mean your child has become a bully. Young individuals from unhappy or financially unstable families are more prone to be bullies because of deep-rooted discontent inside them. Most of the time, their target seems to be other happy kids, i.e., who have what they crave in life. Due to their difficulty fitting in among peers, these individuals often channel their insecurity into attempting to terrorize others. The root of their aggression lies in the frustration they experience, which is then directed at their peers.

The situation must be addressed immediately with therapy or counseling. If something, in particular, is bothering your child, it might come up in therapy sessions with a professional. The child, parents, other family members - and, if possible, the teachers - must be involved in the sessions.

Like neurotypical children, there is a reason behind their bullying tendency; it is the same with ADHD children. Whether it is anger, frustration, or helplessness causing them to act out aggressively, it is not their fault. The entire situation needs to be solved with patience and love.

Your kid has you to help them through their symptoms and limitations at home. Next, they will need to venture into the outside world, where they will face many different people: *people who don't understand their condition, people who don't care about it, and people who don't believe them.*

Chapter 12

The world and universe can be harsh for these children, so you must prepare them to face reality. Outside the house, they will have to learn to live with different types of individuals. Dealing with the rest of the world is a part of their education, and they need to know from you.

"Impossible is just a big word thrown around by small men who find it easier to live in the world they have been given than to explore the power they have to change it. Impossible is not a fact. It's an opinion. Impossible isn't a declaration. It's a dare. Impossible is potential. Impossible is temporary. Impossible is nothing."

— *MUHAMMAD ALI*

13

BONUS CHAPTER
KNOWLEDGE IS POWER

This will be a small chapter, and I want the readers to consider it a list of thoughts I have gathered through the years.

The Illusion of Choice

There is something all parents need to understand: *some things you control as a parent, and others you don't.* Your child will always have two choices, to obey you or not, and it is not much you can do about them. They will likely only follow some of the rules once they are teenagers because that is just the nature of adolescence. This is a psychological game they want to play with their parents to let them know you are not in control of them. It is their way of protesting against your rules, but let's not get into that...

My mother and I have been through something similar in our childhood. She would usually give us an ultimatum instead of a choice, which was quite a usual thing to do in parenting. Let me give you an example. Let's say your child is a little agitated, but you need to leave the house at that very moment; they are not cooperating with you, making you lose your temper. So you scream at them: *"You either come now or I will leave you home!"* not really thinking about the consequences it can cause.

When you deliver an ultimatum like that, you must keep your word. So if you are not okay with having your child stay home, you shouldn't mention it in the first place. Your children will pick on that and think you are often bluffing and not keeping your word. If leaving your child home is an option, you should only give them a choice. So what can you do here that will both control the situation and keep peace with your kid?

What works in these cases is giving your child two choices, but both choices will ultimately lead to the result you want for the scenario. Your child will have two options, giving them the illusion that they are in control when actually, you are in control.

One of the options might be something you know your kid would never want to do, so they have no choice but to choose the one you wanted all along. Something like: *"Either you come with me, or I will carry you out"* Both options lead to what you want, and chances are they don't want to be carried because they think they are mature enough to go by themselves.

Another example is, *"do you want to wear a funny hat or a pair of funny socks when you come with me?"* Whichever they choose, the ending is going to be the same. This method is also known as "The Illusion of Choice," a cognitive bias often used in marketing and advertising. You feel you are in control of choosing what you want, but in reality, you are deciding what the seller wants you to choose. You can also call it a false sense of control; it works daily on adults with marketing people trying to sell you stuff, so imagine the impact it can have on children. Isn't that crazy? It is, but we can use this method to empower our parenting and use it wisely.

Additional Advice for Dealing with ADHD Kids

Just like in a school lesson, we can accidentally not pay attention to the teacher when they are talking about something important or sometimes when we read a paragraph and start thinking about something else until we realize we don't know what this paragraph was about. So I would like to repeat some points mentioned earlier in the book because my goal is that the information sinks in.

♣ *Output equals input. You can only get what you give away.* You'll get good results if you give effort and time.

In real life, the effort brings results. It's the same with your kid. So instead of blaming them, yourself, or your luck or genes, you must put in your best effort in helping them.

♣ *Take care of yourself.* I have already dedicated a chapter to this topic, but I want to repeat it. **Your health and mental well-being are just as important as your child's development.** You need to be at your best to ensure your kid gets your best attention and care.

♣ Please **pay attention to their sleep schedules** and the amount of peaceful sleep they get. This can mean making the house darker and quieter after dusk or turning your screens off for hours before bedtime. It can feel constricting for the parents and the other family members, but these are all necessary steps to ensure your beloved little one gets proper sleep.

♣ **Have faith**! Whether you are a religious person or a spiritual one, I am asking you to have faith. The first step is believing in yourself and your family so things will fall into place.

With the proper treatment, the most severe symptoms will gradually vanish with time; if not, they will still adjust to living with their differences. These kids are usually brilliant; they will sail through even when it is a little more challenging.

♣ **Stay calm**. You are the parent and can't let your child's mood regulate yours. They need you to be calm and in control. They need to be disciplined; they need someone in charge to tell them what to do and guide them.

♣ If your kid is arguing with you, it could be because they need a sense of power temporarily. There is no harm in giving them control back in some situations. So when that happens, **listen instead of arguing** or forcing them to do something. If they decide to skip brushing their teeth one day, ask them why. Instead

Chapter 13

of simply ordering them to do it or assuming they are being argumentative, say something like, "Oh, really? Why do you think you should skip brushing your teeth?" and listen to their side of the story before telling them how they are going to lose their teeth at their thirties if they skip it or don't brush them properly like my mom always told us. It scared me, and we sometimes brushed more than three times daily.

♣ Have you heard of *Bionic Reading*? **Bionic Reading is an app founded in Switzerland that claims to help readers by having the first letters of a word (or algorithmically different) in bold, facilitating the reading and understanding of the written content.** Even though there is no scientific proof for these claims, many neurodiverse people confirm that it does help them. It is possible to try on *Amazon Kindle*, but the process must be done manually. You could speak with your child's teacher and search for the possibilities of using this method on your child's homework. It is possible to import documents into the app. I thought it was more engaging and easier to comprehend.

♣ Successful people swear by this, and you can see this point in almost all of their autobiographies: **teach your children to make their bed first thing in the morning.**

Now, what would this accomplish? It is just one of the dozens of chores your child faces every day, and many times, children don't get the point of it, but it will give them a slight sense of accomplishment as the first task of the day is done. These children live with intense self-doubt; they usually worry about failing at chores and tasks they must complete. Giving them something simple, doable, and easy gives them a positive result less than a few minutes after starting the day, encouraging them to accomplish other tasks later.

You must do the little things right to do the big things right.

This way, they would have already accomplished something when they begin a new day before brushing their teeth.

♣ There are a few apps out there that can come in handy when trying to cope with typical ADHD symptoms, but one that stood out the most to me was *Joon* for children 6 to 12 years old. It is a game that helps to keep your child motivated by developing positive habits like helping with chores and focusing. It teaches them to care for others and develop a sense of independence. It looks entertaining, and parents can create custom tasks for the child. The reward is on the game, so there is less need to buy them things to motivate them, for example. I have no affiliation with the app; it is a clever app that can be a big help.

Remember that absolute consistency is the first thing to get good results. If your child's bedtime is 8:00 pm., make sure your child is in bed at 8:00 pm. every night, with no exceptions. You must deliver it if you warn them of punishment or remove their privileges. Otherwise, they will use your empty words to their advantage, thinking you are bluffing.

Work with their ADHD, and don't try to eliminate it - that should be your mantra. If your kid grows to understand and control it, it becomes their SUPERPOWER!

Something I often recommend to others is to try the Wim Hof Method. It helps tremendously with my symptoms, so you can also look it up online. The Wim Hof Method contains three combined techniques that will achieve excellent results in stress relief, a stronger immune system, better sleep, increased focus, creativity, and willpower. It works! The method combines breathing exercises, cold therapy, and commitment. Have your kid try some of these to see if they can keep up. Adults should supervise children under 16 years old for these methods.

These have all been heartfelt advice I have thought about my whole life and what I have learned from my own experiences and seen from my parents' lives, so I hope they make sense to you.

"Everything will be okay in the end. If it's not okay, it's not the end"

— *JOHN LENNON*

14

CONCLUSION

Children who live with ADHD are different.

Not better or worse than others, just different. Their brains are different; their habits, moods, ideas, ways of perceiving the world, and interactions with others. In a world where they are not the majority, it's easy to misunderstand your child and term them as "lazy," "rude," or "disobedient."

An accurate diagnosis is a wonderful thing. From there, things can only get better because now you understand the reason behind your child's actions, and you can improve your lives by understanding how their brains are wired and by helping them know it to thrive in life.

> *"You've got a Ferrari engine for a brain, and you're lucky, because you're going to win a lot of races. The only problem is, you have bicycle brakes."*
>
> — DR. EDWARD HALLOWELL

What these children need from us - from you and everyone else they look up to, trust, and love - is compassion and support. They need you to understand what they are going through, and they need you to help them to understand it themselves. They need the people they love the most in the world to be a part of this challenging journey they must face every single moment of their lives.

It's difficult for neurotypical brains to understand what happens inside ADHD brains. However, two different types of people can be empathetic to each other, even when they don't understand the reasons behind the differences. By loving your child - not just when they are what you want them to be, but because of who they are - you can be your child's best support in life.

Every kind of love comes with its checklist in this modern day and age. We all want our children to fall into specific categories: *polite, good students, creative, athletic, high achiever, ambitious, and more.* The second our child fails at fulfilling even one of the losses we have created for them, we automatically consider them "lesser than."

This is not our children's fault, but our limitation as a parent. How? When our children fail at something or don't do as well as we want, it's not because they are not trying or good enough. It's because we have never given them a chance to succeed in the past.

When our children are young, most of them show curious minds, always asking "why," "how," and "when" about everything they see. They love to experiment, ask questions, look inside things, or create something new. Most do this because it's how they learn about the world around them.

What do the parents do when their children act like this? Do we encourage them? Do we help them with their curiosity? Most of the time, we stop them from everything. For example, we stop them from experimenting because they are too *loud, messy, nosy, inquisitive, or curious.* We prevent them from expressing themselves because it might mean more work for us or be socially frowned upon. In other words, we rarely allow our kids to be what they

Chapter 14

want to be in their lives, do what they do, and think what they think. The fault lies with us, not them.

If you want them to thrive and grow up as achievers, creators, and entrepreneurs and have thriving careers, it needs to start with you. When you have the right mindset for validating, accepting, acknowledging, and encouraging your ADHD kid, they can embrace their true potential and embody the finest versions of themselves, exactly as they are destined to be.

You will always have to distinguish the best option for your son or daughter and decide the best choice out of your instinct, so believe and trust yourself. Moreover, forgive yourself if you think you have made the wrong decision. I often remind myself that *"every path is the right path,"* meaning every choice you make has a reason why it was chosen.

My ADHD and I

Children with ADHD mostly fail to meet the mental checklist their parents instinctively created for them. As a consequence, they are unable to prevent it from occurring, much like their parents who can't help but feel disappointed in them. This vicious cycle can eradicate relationships, even when the two parties love each other desperately.

I know this because I have experienced, lived through, and survived it all. I have succeeded in finding my way. I have experience. My years living with ADHD have taught me how to survive this disorder as a child, teenager, and adult. It has also given me the courage to write this book. I accepted my ADHD. I unlocked it as I grew up and treated it to this day as my Superpower. I know I am different; I acknowledge that I am unique and thank my ADHD.

There is no use crying over the spilled milk. Things are harder for us than they are for neurotypical people. Most will need help understanding why we can't just do whatever seems more straightforward for them than us. So embrace it and make the best of it!

CONCLUSION

Find your ADHD community. You are not alone! Instead of working harder to achieve something, let's work smarter! We are all different, and we need to find the things that help us the most. Undoubtedly, you must have discovered a wealth of beneficial information within this book. Try them out, step by step, small but definitive, always.

I wish the best for you, your child, and your family! **Remember patience and consistency. If you really want it, you'll get it!** It is the same with your child; they have got to want to get better. You can help them, motivate them. The change starts with those who want to see the difference. Since your child is too young to understand, you need to explain how important it is for them to understand their own brain and work with it. I will finish this chapter with a saying my dad always told my brother and me, which stuck with me because of its power.

*"It's **not who you think you are** that stops you from achieving your goals.*

*It's **whom you think you are not** that stops you from achieving your goals."*

Take Away from the Book

What did I want to share with this book that has taken me years to write? In a nutshell, everything I know, experienced, and have learned and researched. You can find everything you need about this disorder in this book. Not just everything you can research yourself on the Internet but also what my years have taught me. *Just as your child's physician can prescribe the correct medicine, your therapist can guide them in learning necessary social and coping skills.* My book will help you - the parents, guardians, and well-wishers - to help your loved little one sail through this condition.

I have lived as a neurodivergent individual and have seen my parents struggle. So I know exactly what kind of information or assurance parents and guardians need at these moments. There is no shame in asking for help when you need it, especially from someone who understands and has been through all of it. I am confident you have found valuable new information in this book, and I am happy to share it with you.

Thank you!

PLEASE REVIEW MY BOOK
YOU CAN MAKE A DIFFERENCE

Thank you for taking the time to read my book. Writing and publishing this book has been a labor of love, and I am grateful for every reader who chooses to spend their time with my words.

If you enjoyed it, please consider leaving a review on the platform where you purchased it. Your review can help other readers decide whether this book is worth their time and money. But, more importantly, your review can also help me as an author. **Reviews are one of the most powerful tools** to help authors connect with readers, improve their writing, and promote their books.

If you have a busy schedule at the moment, I would be truly grateful if you could leave at least a rating. It can make a big difference, and I promise to read and appreciate each one.

I hope to hear from you soon.

Sincerely,

Renato Flauzino

If you would like to contact me, my email is:
info@novomundopublishing.com

Please Review My Book

Scan this QR Code below to conveniently access my book in your local Amazon Store and save yourself some valuable time.

Also, please consider leaving a like on our Facebook Page, where we provide advice, tricks, and tips for managing ADHD symptoms across all ages.

ACKNOWLEDGMENTS

Special Thanks to the ADHD Community
We have a worldwide ADHD community that provides mutual support and guidance on how to deal with the challenges we encounter every day. I am grateful for their assistance and encouragement in managing our diverse symptoms. Although there are numerous other resources available, these are the ones that I am most in contact with.

- ADDitude - Team
- ADHD Diversified - MJ Siemens
- ADHD Rewired - Eric Tivers, Kat Hoyer
- ADHD Essentials - Brendan Mahan
- Hacking your ADHD - William Curb
- How to ADHD - Jessica McCabe and team
- Live on Purpose Tv - Dr. Paul Jenkins
- Optimal Mind Performance - Dr. LeGrand Peterson

REFERENCES

Aggarwal, S. (2021, November 21). *30 Ways to Be a More Fun, Playful Parent.* KidPillar. https://kidpillar.com/ways-fun-playful-parents/

Alexis, A., C., (2022b, March 7). *Can Children Drink Kombucha?* Healthline. https://www.healthline.com/nutrition/can-children-drink-kombucha#bottom-line

American Psychiatric Association. *APA - Frequently Asked Questions.* (n.d.). https://www.psychiatry.org/psychiatrists/practice/dsm/feedback-and-questions/frequently-asked-questions#:

Anderson, D., (2023, March 3). *What is the difference between ADD and ADHD?* Child Mind Institute. https://childmind.org/article/what-is-the-difference-between-add-and-adhd/#:

Anderson, D., (2023, March 3). *What is the difference between ADD and ADHD?* Child Mind Institute. https://childmind.org/article/what-is-the-difference-between-add-and-adhd/#:

Arabi, S., MA. (2022, July 1). *All About Equine Assisted Psychotherapy.* Psych Central. https://psychcentral.com/health/equine-assisted-psychotherapy

Arjmand, H., Hohagen, J., Paton, B., & Rickard, N. S. (2017). Emotional Responses to Music: Shifts in Frontal Brain Asymmetry Mark Periods of Musical Change. *Frontiers in Psychology*, 8. https://doi.org/10.3389/fpsyg.2017.02044

Barkley, R., & ADDitude Editors. (2023c, February 23). *ADHD Treatment: Medication, Diet, Therapy & More Options.* ADDitude. https://www.additudemag.com/how-to-treat-adhd-with-medication-therapy-food-coaching/

Battista V., Philadelphia, C. H. O.P. (2018, March 6). *How Aromatherapy Can Help Children.* Children's Hospital of Philadelphia. https://www.chop.edu/news/health-tip/how-aromatherapy-can-help-children#:

Belliveau, J. (2018, September 2). *ADHD Rating Scales: What You Need to Know.* Healthline. https://www.healthline.com/health/adhd/rating-scale

Benton, David. "Dehydration Influences Mood and Cognition: A Plausible Hypothesis?" *Nutrients*, vol. 3, no. 5, 10 May 2011, pp. 555–573, https://doi.org/10.3390/nu3050555

Black, M. M. (2003). Micronutrient Deficiencies and Cognitive Functioning. *Journal of Nutrition*, 133(11), S3927–S3931. https://doi.org/10.1093/jn/133.11.3927s

Braaten, E., Brown, T. E., Cunningham, B. (2017, April 24). *Large-Scale MRI Study Confirms ADHD Brain Differences | Understood.* Understood. https://www.understood.org/articles/large-scale-mri-study-confirms-adhd-brain-differences

Brown T. E. (2021, January 29). *At What Age Can ADHD Be Diagnosed? | Understood.* https://www.understood.org/en/articles/when-can-adhd-be-diagnosed-in-children

Brown, T., E., *At What Age Can ADHD Be Diagnosed? | Understood.* (2021, January 29). Understood. https://www.understood.org/en/articles/when-can-adhd-be-diagnosed-in-children

References

Butje, A., Repede, E., & Shattell, M. (2008). Healing Scents: An Overview of Clinical Aromatherapy for Emotional Distress. *Journal of Psychosocial Nursing and Mental Health Services, 46*(10), 46–52. https://doi.org/10.3928/02793695-20081001-12

Cafasso, J. (2021, SNovember 5). *Do Binaural Beats Have Health Benefits?* Healthline. https://www.healthline.com/health/binaural-beats

Caron Treatment Centers. (2022, April 12). *What Does Adderall Do to Your Brain? It Depends | Caron.* https://www.caron.org/blog/what-does-adderall-do-to-your-brain-it-depends

Center on the Developing Child at Harvard University. (2020, March 24). *Executive Function & Self-Regulation.* https://developingchild.harvard.edu/science/key-concepts/executive-function/

Center on the Developing Child at Harvard University. (2020b, March 24). *Executive Function & Self-Regulation.* https://developingchild.harvard.edu/science/key-concepts/executive-function/

Centers for Disease Control and Prevention. (2020, September 21). *Treatment of ADHD | CDC.* https://www.cdc.gov/ncbddd/adhd/treatment.html

Centers for Disease Control and Prevention. (2021, January 26). *What is ADHD? CDC.* https://www.cdc.gov/ncbddd/adhd/facts.html#ref

Centers for Disease Control and Prevention. (2022, June 8). *Data and Statistics About ADHD | CDC.* https://www.cdc.gov/ncbddd/adhd/data.html#:

Chafin, S., Roy, M. J., Gerin, W., & Christenfeld, N. (2004). Music can facilitate blood pressure recovery from stress. *British Journal of Health Psychology, 9*(3), 393–403. https://doi.org/10.1348/1359107041557020

Chen, H., Yang, Y., Odisho, D., Wu, S., Yi, C., & Oliver, B. G. (2023). Can biomarkers be used to diagnose attention deficit hyperactivity disorder? *Frontiers in Psychiatry, 14.* https://doi.org/10.3389/fpsyt.2023.1026616

Cherry, K. (2022, November 8). *What Is Behavioral Therapy?* Verywell Mind. http://verywellmind.com/what-is-behavioral-therapy-2795998

Cherry, K. (2022a, August 10). *What Is Cognitive Behavioral Therapy (CBT)?* Verywell Mind. https://www.verywellmind.com/what-is-cognitive-behavior-therapy-2795747

Children and Adults with Attention Deficit/Hyperactivity Disorder. (2018, October 23). *More Fire Than Water: A Short History of ADHD - CHADD.* https://chadd.org/adhd-weekly/more-fire-than-water-a-short-history-of-adhd/

Children and Adults with Attention Deficit/Hyperactivity Disorder. (2019, June 13) *- About ADHD - Symptoms, Causes and Treatment -.* CHADD. https://chadd.org/about-adhd/overview/#:

Children and Adults with Attention Deficit/Hyperactivity Disorder. (2020, October 6). *Diagnosing ADHD - CHADD.* https://chadd.org/about-adhd/diagnosing-adhd/

Clarke, J.,(2022, December 3). *How Is ADHD Severity Measured?* Verywell Mind. https://www.verywellmind.com/how-is-adhd-severity-measured-5496273

Conger K., *Herbs for ADHD.* (2020, September 29). Remedy Holistic. https://www.remedyrx.com/blogs/the-remedy-blog/herbs-for-adhd

References

Coppola, F., (n.d.). *ADHD & Executive Function*. Debbie Tracht Coaching. http://www.middleburycenter.com/adhd-and-executive-function.html

De Marco, K., Buck, P. W., Bean, N., (2017). Equine-Assisted Psychotherapy: An Emerging Trauma-Informed Intervention. *Advances in Social Work, 18*(1), 387–402. https://doi.org/10.18060/21310

Dodson, W., & ADDitude Editors. (2023b, February 23). *ADHD Treatment: Medication, Diet, Therapy & More Options*. ADDitude. https://www.additudemag.com/how-to-treat-adhd-with-medication-therapy-food-coaching/

Dodson, W., & ADDitude Editors. (2023d, February 23). *ADHD Treatment: Medication, Diet, Therapy & More Options*. ADDitude. https://www.additudemag.com/how-to-treat-adhd-with-medication-therapy-food-coaching/

Dodson, W., M.D., ADDitude Editors. (2023, February 23). *ADHD Treatment: Medication, Diet, Therapy & More Options*. ADDitude. https://www.additudemag.com/how-to-treat-adhd-with-medication-therapy-food-coaching/#footnote2.

Drugs.com. (n.d.-b) *How long does Adderall stay in your system (urine drug test)?* https://www.drugs.com/medical-answers/long-adderall-stay-system-urine-drug-test-663004/

DSM-5-TR. Facts About *DSM-5-TR*. (2022). *Psychiatric News, 57*(3). https://doi.org/10.1176/appi.pn.2022.03.3.28

Durbin, K., *Adderall: Uses, Dosage, Side Effects & Safety Info*. (n.d.). Drugs.com. https://www.drugs.com/adderall.html#.

Faraone, S. V. (2003b, June 1). *The worldwide prevalence of ADHD: is it an American condition?* PubMed Central (PMC). https://www.ncbi.nlm.nih.gov/pmc/articles/PMC1525089/

Furman, L. (2005). What Is Attention-Deficit Hyperactivity Disorder (ADHD)? *Journal of Child Neurology, 20*(12), 994–1002. https://doi.org/10.1177/08830738050200121301

Ginapp, C. M., Angarita, G. A., Bold, K. W., & Potenza, M. N. (2022). The lived experiences of adults with attention-deficit/hyperactivity disorder: A rapid review of qualitative evidence. *Frontiers in Psychiatry, 13*. https://doi.org/10.3389/fpsyt.2022.949321

Golden, M. (2021, April 8). *A Simple Exercise to Stimulate Your Cerebellum and Boost Your Movement Accuracy, Balance, and Coordination - MedFitNetwork*. MedFitNetwork. https://medfitnetwork.org/public/all-mfn/a-simple-exercise-to-stimulate-your-cerebellum-and-boost-your-movement-accuracy-balance-and-coordination/

Gotter, A. (2018, September 29). *Behavioral Therapy*. Healthline. https://www.healthline.com/health/behavioral-therapy

Greenblatt, J., M., M.D. (2022, April 20). *How Pine Bark Extract (Pycnogenol) Can Help ADHD - Finally Focused*. Finally Focused. https://finallyfocused.org/how-pine-bark-extract-pycnogenol-can-help-regulate-adhd-symptoms/

Gunnerson, T. (2020, July 13). *A Brief History of ADHD*. WebMD. https://www.webmd.com/add-adhd/adhd-history#:

Gupta, M., Singh, M., & Students, C. (2017, August 12). *The use of Brahmi for Attention-Deficit/Hyperactivity Disorder (ADHD) in Children: A Review By Deborah

References

Berger. California College of Ayurveda. https://www.ayurvedacollege.com/blog/brahmi-review/

Hallowell, E., (2022, January 10). *ADHD Needs a Better Name. We Have One.* ADDitude. https://www.additudemag.com/attention-deficit-disorder-vast/#:

Harmat, L., Takács, J., & Bódizs, R. (2008). Music improves sleep quality in students. *Journal of Advanced Nursing, 62*(3), 327–335. https://doi.org/10.1111/j.1365-2648.2008.04602.x..

Hasan, S. H. (2018, March). *ADHD Medicines.* Nemours KidsHealth. Retrieved April 10, 2023. *https://kidshealth.org/en/teens/ritalin.html#:*

Heal, D. J., Smith, S. M., Gosden, J., & Nutt, D. J. (2013). Amphetamine, past and present – a pharmacological and clinical perspective. *Journal of Psychopharmacology, 27*(6), 479–496. https://doi.org/10.1177/0269881113482532

Holland, T. M., (2018, April 28) *Facts About Touch: How Human Contact Affects Your Health and Relationships.* https://www.dignityhealth.org/articles/facts-about-touch-how-human-contact-affects-your-health-and-relationships

Hoogman, M., Bralten, J., Hibar, D. P., Mennes, M., Zwiers, M. P., Schweren, L. J. S., Van Hulzen, K. J. E., McIntosh, A. M., Shumskaya, E., Jahanshad, N., De Zeeuw, P., Szekely, E., Sudre, G., Wolfers, T., Onnink, A. M. H., Dammers, J., Mostert, J. C., Vives-Gilabert, Y., Kohls, G., . . . Franke, B. (2017). Subcortical brain volume differences in participants with attention deficit hyperactivity disorder in children and adults: a cross-sectional mega-analysis. *The Lancet Psychiatry, 4*(4), 310–319. https://doi.org/10.1016/s2215-0366(17)30049-4

Hoza, B., Smith, A. D., Shoulberg, E. K., Linnea, K., Dorsch, T. E., Blazo, J. A., Alerding, C. M., & McCabe, G. P. (2015). A Randomized Trial Examining the Effects of Aerobic Physical Activity on Attention-Deficit/Hyperactivity Disorder Symptoms in Young Children. *Journal of Abnormal Child Psychology, 43*(4), 655–667. https://doi.org/10.1007/s10802-014-9929-y
https://kidshealth.org/en/teens/ritalin.html#:

Huberman, A. (2022, December 12). *ADHD & How Anyone Can Improve Their Focus.* Huberman Lab. https://hubermanlab.com/adhd-and-how-anyone-can-improve-their-focus/.

Huberman, A. (2022, December 12). *ADHD & How Anyone Can Improve Their Focus.* Huberman Lab. https://hubermanlab.com/adhd-and-how-anyone-can-improve-their-focus/

Hyde, K. L., Lerch, J. P., Norton, A., Forgeard, M. J. C., Winner, E., Evans, A. C., & Schlaug, G. (2009). Musical Training Shapes Structural Brain Development. *The Journal of Neuroscience, 29*(10), 3019–3025. https://doi.org/10.1523/jneurosci.5118-08.2009

Johansen-Berg, H. (2009, October 12) *Juggling enhances connections in the brain | University of Oxford.* https://www.ox.ac.uk/news/2009-10-12-juggling-enhances-connections-brain

Juergens, J. (2023, February 21). *Adderall Addiction And Abuse - Addiction Center.* Addiction Center. https://www.addictioncenter.com/stimulants/adderall/

Juggling Balls Australia (n.d.). *- 16 Amazing Benefits of Juggling* https://www.jugglingballs.com.au/16-benefits-of-juggling/.

Kanduri, C., Raijas, P., Ahvenainen, M., Philips, A. K., Ukkola-Vuoti, L.,

References

Lähdesmäki, H., & Järvelä, I. (2015). The effect of listening to music on human transcriptome. *PeerJ, 3*, e830. https://doi.org/10.7717/peerj.830

Kennedy, D. N., Bonnländer, B., Lang, S. C., Pischel, I., Forster, J., Khan, J., Jackson, P. A., & Wightman, E. L. (2020). Acute and Chronic Effects of Green Oat (Avena sativa) Extract on Cognitive Function and Mood during a Laboratory Stressor in Healthy Adults: A Randomised, Double-Blind, Placebo-Controlled Study in Healthy Humans. *Nutrients, 12*(6), 1598. https://doi.org/10.3390/nu12061598

Kerna, N. A., Flores, J., Holets, H. M., & Kadivi, K. (2020). Adderall: On the Razor's Edge of ADHD Treatment, Enhanced Academic and Physical Performance, Addiction,. . . *ResearchGate*. https://doi.org/10.31080/ecpp.2020.09.00801

Kuratko, C. N., Barrett, E. C., Nelson, E., & Salem, N. (2013). The Relationship of Docosahexaenoic Acid (DHA) with Learning and Behavior in Healthy Children: A Review. *Nutrients, 5*(7), 2777–2810. https://doi.org/10.3390/nu5072777

Layton, T. J., Barnett, M., Hicks, T. R., & Jena, A. B. (2018). Attention Deficit–Hyperactivity Disorder and Month of School Enrollment. *The New England Journal of Medicine, 379*(22), 2122–2130. https://doi.org/10.1056/nejmoa1806828

Learning Assessment and Neurocare Centre, Learning Assessment and. "NUTRITION and EXERCISE." *Https://Www.lanc.org.uk/Wp-Content/Uploads/2013/01/Nutrition-And-Exercise-Full-Handout.pdf*, 2013

Lee, S., Park, W. H., & Lim, M. H. (2011). Clinical Effects of Korean Red Ginseng on Attention Deficit Hyperactivity Disorder in Children: An Observational Study. *Journal of Ginseng Research, 35*(2), 226–234. https://doi.org/10.5142/jgr.2011.35.2.226

Leitner, Y. (2014). The Co-Occurrence of Autism and Attention Deficit Hyperactivity Disorder in Children â€" What Do We Know? *Frontiers in Human Neuroscience, 8*. https://doi.org/10.3389/fnhum.2014.00268

Marshall-Pescini, S., Schaebs, F. S., Gaugg, A., Meinert, A., Deschner, T., & Range, F. (2019). The Role of Oxytocin in the Dog–Owner Relationship. *Animals, 9*(10), 792. https://doi.org/10.3390/ani9100792

Martin, C. (2022, October 27). *What Is the Difference Between a Disease and a Disorder?* Verywell Health. https://www.verywellhealth.com/disease-vs-disorder-5092243

Marzbani, H., Marateb, H. R., & Mansourian, M. (2016). Methodological Note: Neurofeedback: A Comprehensive Review on System Design, Methodology and Clinical Applications. *Basic and Clinical Neuroscience, 7*(2). https://doi.org/10.15412/j.bcn.03070208

Mason, O., Rosier, T., (2022, January 19). *Face It — People with ADHD Are Wired Differently*. ADDitude. https://www.additudemag.com/current-research-on-adhd-breakdown-of-the-adhd-brain/

McCarthy, C., MD. (2019, January 1). *The better way to discipline children*. Harvard Health https://www.health.harvard.edu/blog/the-better-way-to-discipline-children-2019010115578.

McCarthy, L. F. (2023, February 8). *ADHD Medications for Children*. ADDitude. https://www.additudemag.com/adhd-medications-for-children/

McQueen, J. (2022, June 3). *Childhood ADHD and Screen Time*. WebMD. https://www.webmd.com/add-adhd/childhood-adhd/childhood-adhd-screen-time

Melby-Lervåg, M., & Hulme, C. (2013). Is working memory training effective? A

References

meta-analytic review. *Developmental Psychology, 49*(2), 270–291. https://doi.org/10.1037/a0028228

Mercuri, M., Sheth, T., & Natarajan, M. K. (2011). Radiation exposure from medical imaging: A silent harm? *Canadian Medical Association Journal, 183*(4), 413–414. https://doi.org/10.1503/cmaj.101885

Michaels, P. (2022, March 31). *Brain Training for ADHD: What Is It? Does It Work?* ADDitude. https://www.additudemag.com/adhd-brain-training-neurofeedback-memory/

Michaels, P. (2022, March 31). *Brain Training for ADHD: What Is It? Does It Work?* ADDitude. https://www.additudemag.com/adhd-brain-training-neurofeedback-memory/.

Morin, A. (2021, January 14). *History of Learning Disabilities and ADHD | Understood*. Understood. https://www.understood.org/en/articles/history-of-learning-disabilities-and-adhd

Moukhtarian, T. R., Mintah, R. S., Moran, P., & Asherson, P. (2018). Emotion dysregulation in attention-deficit/hyperactivity disorder and borderline personality disorder. *Borderline Personality Disorder and Emotion Dysregulation, 5*(1). https://doi.org/10.1186/s40479-018-0086-8

Myers, W. (2018, January 10). *7 Foods to Avoid If Your Child Has ADHD*. EverydayHealth.com. http://everydayhealth.com/adhd-pictures/how-food-can-affect-your-childs-adhd-symptoms.aspx#:

Naidoo., U., (2020, September 1). *Can what you eat worsen your ADHD?* KevinMD.com. https://www.kevinmd.com/2020/08/can-what-you-eat-worsen-your-adhd.html

Nair, M. (2022, December 12). *Learn About the Stories of 8 of the World's Most Successful People with ADHD*. University of the People. https://www.uopeople.edu/blog/8-of-the-worlds-most-successful-people-with-adhd/

NeuroHealth Associates. (2020, November 10). *The 9 Best Treatments for Children and Adults with ADHD*. https://nhahealth.com/the-9-best-treatments-for-children-and-adults-with-adhd/#:

NeuroHealth Associates. (2020b, November 10). *The 9 Best Treatments for Children and Adults with ADHD*. https://nhahealth.com/the-9-best-treatments-for-children-and-adults-with-adhd/#:

Newmark, S., MD. (2023a, February 8). *Eggs, Dairy, Nuts, and Soy: Testing for Food Sensitivities with an ADHD Elimination Diet*. ADDitude. https://www.additudemag.com/testing-for-food-sensitivities-in-children-with-adhd/

Nissley-Tsiopinis, J., Normand, S., Mautone, J. A., Fogler, J. M., Featherston, M., & Power, T. J. (2022). Preparing Families for Evidence-Based Treatment of ADHD: Development of Bootcamp for ADHD. *Cognitive and Behavioral Practice*. https://doi.org/10.1016/j.cbpra.2022.02.022

Park, C., & Son, H. (2022). Immediate Effects of Fine-Motor Training on Coordination and Dexterity of the Non-Dominant Hand in Healthy Adults: A Randomized Controlled Trial. *Behavioral Sciences, 12*(11), 446. https://doi.org/10.3390/bs12110446

Pedersen, T. (2021, April 15). *Treatment of ADHD in Children and Teens*. Psych

References

Central. https://psychcentral.com/childhood-adhd/treatment-of-adhd-in-children

Ponnou, S., & Thomé, B. (2022). ADHD diagnosis and methylphenidate consumption in children and adolescents: A systematic analysis of health databases in France over the period 2010–2019. *Frontiers in Psychiatry, 13*. https://doi.org/10.3389/fpsyt.2022.957242

Raman, R. Rd, M.S. (2019, November 1). *7 Emerging Benefits of Bacopa monnieri (Brahmi)*. Healthline. https://www.healthline.com/nutrition/bacopa-monnieri-benefits.

Rawe, J. (2022, February 2). *The ADHD Brain | Understood*. Understood. https://www.understood.org/articles/en/adhd-and-the-brain

Rodgers, A. L. (2022, November 29). *New Finding: ADHD Medication Not Associated with Cardiovascular Risk at Any Age*. ADDitude. https://www.additudemag.com/adhd-medication-no-cardiovascular-risk-hypertension-heart-failure/

Rossi, A., Molinaro, A., Savi, E., Micheletti, S., Galli, J., Chirico, G., & Rossi, D. (2018). Music reduces pain perception in healthy newborns: A comparison between different music tracks and recoded heartbeat. *Early Human Development, 124*, 7–10. https://doi.org/10.1016/j.earlhumdev.2018.07.006

Rowe, S. (2021, April 7). *Could My Child Have ADHD?* Psych Central. https://psychcentral.com/childhood-adhd/childhood-teenager-adhd-symptoms

Russo, A. (2023, January 22). *ADD vs. ADHD Symptoms: 3 Types of Attention Deficit Disorder*. ADDitude. https://www.additudemag.com/add-adhd-symptoms-difference/#footnote2

Ryu, S. J., Choi, Y., An, H., Kwon, H., Ha, M., Hong, Y., Hong, S., & Hwang, H. (2022). Associations between Dietary Intake and Attention Deficit Hyperactivity Disorder (ADHD) Scores by Repeated Measurements in School-Age Children. *Nutrients, 14*(14), 2919. https://doi.org/10.3390/nu14142919

Sachdev, P. (2021, September 07) - *The Brain on ADHD*. WebMD. https://www.webmd.com/add-adhd/video/brain-adhd.

Sachdev, P., (n.d.). *The Brain on ADHD*. WebMD. https://www.webmd.com/add-adhd/video/brain-adhd

Saline S. & ADDitude Editors. (2022, September 6). *10 Commonly Misdiagnosed ADHD Symptoms*. ADDitude. https://www.additudemag.com/slideshows/adhd-misdiagnosis/

Santos, L., Fernández-Río, J., Fernández-García, B., Jakobsen, M. D., González-Gómez, L., & Suman, O. E. (2016). Effects of Slackline Training on Postural Control, Jump Performance, and Myoelectrical Activity in Female Basketball Players. *Journal of Strength and Conditioning Research, 30*(3), 653–664. https://doi.org/10.1519/jsc.0000000000001168

Seay, B. (2023, January 21). *Your Complete ADHD Diagnosis and Testing Guide*. ADDitude. https://www.additudemag.com/adhd-testing-diagnosis-guide/

Seay, B., Ratey, N., (2023b, January 22). *The ADHD-Dopamine Link: Why You Crave Sugar and Carbs*. ADDitude. https://www.additudemag.com/slideshows/adhd-obesity-link/#:

Shanker, T., Duenwald M. (2003, January 19). *The New York Times - THREATS AND RESPONSES: MILITARY; Bombing Error Puts a Spotlight On Pilots' Pills*. The New

References

York Times. https://www.nytimes.com/2003/01/19/us/threats-and-responses-military-bombing-error-puts-a-spotlight-on-pilots-pills.html

Sinfield, J. (2022, November 14). *The ADHD vs. Non-ADHD Brain*. Verywell Mind. https://www.verywellmind.com/the-adhd-brain-4129396

Slobodin, O., & Davidovitch, M. (2019). Gender Differences in Objective and Subjective Measures of ADHD Among Clinic-Referred Children. *Frontiers in Human Neuroscience, 13*. https://doi.org/10.3389/fnhum.2019.00441

Slobodin, O., Davidovitch, M. (2019). Gender Differences in Objective and Subjective Measures of ADHD Among Clinic-Referred Children. *Frontiers in Human Neuroscience, 13*. https://doi.org/10.3389/fnhum.2019.00441

Sonne, J. (2022, July 4). *Dopamine*. StatPearls - NCBI Bookshelf. https://www.ncbi.nlm.nih.gov/books/NBK535451/

Speyer, L. G., Eisner, M., Ribeaud, D., Luciano, M., Auyeung, B., & Murray, A. L. (2021). Developmental Relations Between Internalising Problems and ADHD in Childhood: a Symptom Level Perspective. *Research on Child and Adolescent Psychopathology, 49*(12), 1567–1579. https://doi.org/10.1007/s10802-021-00856-3

Sprinkle, N. (2021, May 7). *Behavioral Therapy for ADHD: A Pragmatic Parent's Guide*. ADDitude. https://www.additudemag.com/behavior-therapy-it-works/

Staffordshire County Council *Dehydration and older people (detailed factsheet) -*. (n.d.). https://www.staffordshire.gov.uk/Advice-support-and-care-for-adults/Help-and-support-with-daily-living/Eating-and-drinking/Dehydration-and-older-people-detailed-factsheet.aspx#:

Stevens, L., (2022, October 26). *The Sugar Wars: How Food Impacts ADHD Symptoms*. ADDitude. https://www.additudemag.com/sugar-diet-nutrition-impact-adhd-symptoms/

Tartakovsky M., MS, (2021b, August 17). *Why Is My ADHD So Bad Today and What Can I Do?* Psych Central. https://psychcentral.com/adhd/my-adhd-is-so-bad-today

The American Psychiatric Association. *APA - DSM History*. (n.d.). https://www.psychiatry.org/psychiatrists/practice/dsm/history-of-the-dsm

The Healthline Editorial Team. (2023, March 8). *ADHD Treatment Options: Therapy, Medication, and More*. Healthline. https://www.healthline.com/health/adhd/treatment-overview#1

The National Health Service Website, N. (2022, January 12). *Diagnosis*. nhs.uk. https://www.nhs.uk/conditions/attention-deficit-hyperactivity-disorder-adhd/diagnosis/#:

The National Institute on Drug Abuse, (2021, June 24). *How Does Adderall Make You Feel if You Don't Have ADHD?* Evoke Wellness Corporate. https://evokewellness.com/blog/how-adderall-make-feel-dont-have-adhd/.

The Zen Studies Society (n.d.). *What Is Zen?* Zen Studies. https://zenstudies.org/teachings/what-is-zen/

Timothy, J., L., & The Healthline Editorial Team. (2018b, July 25). *Supplements to Treat ADHD*. Healthline. https://www.healthline.com/health/adhd/treatments-supplements

U.S. Geological Survey (2019, October 22).| *The Water in You: Water and the Human*

References

Body https://www.usgs.gov/special-topics/water-science-school/science/water-you-water-and-human-body#overview.

Utz, J., (2000, May 15). *Re: What percentage of the human body is composed of water?* https://www.madsci.org/posts/archives/may2000/958588306.An.r.html

Van Dorn, A. (2023). The strange endurance of corporal punishment. *The Lancet Child & Adolescent Health, 7*(3), 154–155. https://doi.org/10.1016/s2352-4642(23)00019-6

Vieyra, M. & AAWE Guide to Education in France, (2022, February 27). *Attention Deficit/Hyperactivity Disorder (ADHD) – Part 2.* https://www.aaweparis.org/2022/02/23/attention-deficit-hyperactivity-disorder-adhd-part-2/

Weyandt, L. L., White, T. L., Gudmundsdottir, B. G., Nitenson, A. Z., Rathkey, E. S., De Leon, K. A., & Bjorn, S. A. (2018). Neurocognitive, Autonomic, and Mood Effects of Adderall: A Pilot Study of Healthy College Students. *Pharmacy, 6*(3), 58. https://doi.org/10.3390/pharmacy6030058

White, E. (2023, March 21). *My Child Was Diagnosed with ADHD, Now What?* Buzzrx.com. https://www.buzzrx.com/blog/my-child-was-diagnosed-with-adhd-now-what.

White, H. A. (2020). Thinking "Outside the Box": Unconstrained Creative Generation in Adults with Attention Deficit Hyperactivity Disorder. *Journal of Creative Behavior, 54*(2), 472–483. https://doi.org/10.1002/jocb.382

Wilens, T., (2023, February 8). *Does Stimulant Medication Cause Drug Dependence?* ADDitude. https://www.additudemag.com/adhd-stimulant-medication-addiction-side-effects/

Williams, L., (2020, May 30). *The Health and Fitness Benefits of Slacklining.* Verywell Fit. https://www.verywellfit.com/the-health-and-fitness-benefits-of-slacklining-3879767

Wright, R. (2022, June 2). *Why ADHD Misdiagnoses Can Be Common.* Psych Central. https://psychcentral.com/adhd/adhd-misdiagnosis

Yates, Allison A. "Report Sets Dietary Intake Levels for Water, Salt, and Potassium to Maintain Health and Reduce Chronic Disease Risk." *Nationalacademies.org*, 11 Feb. 2004, www.nationalacademies.org/news/2004/02/report-sets-dietary-intake-levels-for-water-salt-and-potassium-to-maintain-health-and-reduce-chronic-disease-risk

Printed in Great Britain
by Amazon